When Ads Work

New Proof that Advertising Triggers Sales

John Philip Jones

LEXINGTON BOOKS
An Imprint of The Free Press
New York London Toronto Sydney Tokyo Singapore

Library of Congress Cataloging-in-Publication Data

Jones, John Philip.
    When ads work : new proof that advertising triggers sales / John
Philip Jones.
        p.   cm.
    Includes index.
    ISBN 0-02-916662-4
    1. Advertising—Case studies.   2. Sales promotion—Case studies.
    I. Title.
HF5823.J719   1995
659.1—dc20   94-24948
                                                                     CIP

Lexington Books
An Imprint of The Free Press
A Division of Simon & Schuster Inc.
1230 Avenue of the Americas
New York, N. Y. 10020

Printed in the United States of America

printing number

1 2 3 4 5 6 7 8 9 10

To Dennis Tobolski, Patrick Kung, and Vincent Wong

Practical experience in itself is of little use unless it forms the basis of reflection and thought.
—Bernard Law Montgomery

Contents

List of Tables and Figures

Tables

Figures

Preface

When *Ads Work* describes new research and it publishes many facts. There are very few theories, and those few are all rooted in the facts. The data in this book are derived from single-source research, the most accurate system yet developed for measuring the sales effects of advertising. The book addresses the fundamental question of how advertising influences sales.

I processed much of the statistical information and wrote a pilot report almost a year before I began to write the text of the book. This time was occupied with reflection. I also discussed the pilot report with a number of people who had something to contribute—experienced advertising, marketing, and research practitioners in the United States and abroad. These practitioners have inevitably influenced my interpretation of the facts. To an even greater degree, my interpretation has been conditioned by my own professional experience, derived largely although not exclusively from large brands. This interaction of facts, experience, discussion, and thought is the reason I chose to begin this book with the aphorism, written by the famous soldier Bernard Law Montgomery.[1]

The advertising business has a poor track record in providing reliable knowledge of its processes and effects. We know little about what proportion of campaigns work, and about the meaning of short-term success; even less about long-term success, and how the short term and the long term are related to each other. If we know too little about advertising's payout in sales, we know even less about its return in terms of profit. We have a very patchy understanding of the connection between advertising's influence (if any) on behavior, on knowledge, and on attitudes. We have a very inadequate knowledge of how to calculate the optimal advertising budget for a brand and how to deploy this budget most efficiently in media plans.

This is not the end of the deplorable list of things about which we know too little. But I am encouraged enough to believe—and I hope readers will soon agree—that the facts in this book generate much light that can be beamed into some of the dark corners. This book is much concerned with five substantial discoveries, which will shortly be described,

This book is organized into *Part 1: Five Discoveries, Part 2: Evidence for Part One—Seventy-Eight Brands Dissected*, and a number of Appendices. This organization was dictated by the fact that the book is addressed to two groups of people.

One group is the users of advertising: executives at all levels on the marketing side of manufacturing companies, and in agencies. These people—the advertising/marketing generalists and the media specialists—will be concerned mainly with the lessons in Part 1, although they will also need reassurance, provided by other parts of the book, that these lessons are well founded.

The lessons in Part 1 are intended to enable advertisers to reap a double benefit: to their brands' sales and to their own overall financial performance (which is sure to result from their making more efficient use of their advertising budgets).

The second group of people are market research practitioners, as much concerned with the supporting evidence as with the specific recommendations for marketing brands. Researchers will scrutinize Part 2 and the six Appendices with special care; in particular my description of the checkered history of single-source research and the reasons its promise has not until now been fulfilled (see Appendices B and C).

Part 2 contains a fairly large amount of statistical data, but I have presented these facts in a way that nonspecialist readers can understand. The chapters in Part 1 contain references to chapters in Part 2, so that readers can immediately study any particular topic in more depth.

The Structure of the Book

Part 1—Five Discoveries

Chapters 2 through 6 describe the five most salient conclusions from this research:

Chapter 2 shows how pure single-source research is used to measure the short-term effect of advertising, using a measure entitled Short-Term Advertising Strength (STAS). It details the range of short-term responses, calculated for the brands covered by the research.

Chapter 3 estimates the proportion of brands for which advertising generates a positive short-term effect, and the proportion for which advertising also works in the long term; and it compares the performance of advertised and unadvertised brands.

Chapter 4 demonstrates that one exposure of an effective campaign is all you need to generate an immediate effect; this chapter focuses on the most important factor influencing the deployment of media dollars.

Chapter 5 demonstrates the high degree of synergy that can operate between advertising and promotions.

Chapter 6 demonstrates how advertising actually works in the short and long term, and is intended to improve the efficiency of the advertising industry in planning and writing campaigns.

Chapter 7 is an interlude. This chapter is not based on quantitative research. It is devoted to my own inferences about the most important characteristics of advertising campaigns that are most successful in the short and long term—and how these characteristics were identified in the writings of the best-known advertising practitioners.

Part 2—Evidence for Part 1:
Seventy-eight Brands Dissected

This part is devoted to an analysis of the brands studied in this research, organized as follows:

Chapter 8 discusses Alpha One brands; advertising that works.

Chapter 9 covers Alpha Two brands; advertising that stops working.

Chapter 10 explores Beta brands; advertising that works in some cases.

Chapter 11 talks about Gamma brands; advertising that does not work.

Chapter 12 examines the underlying patterns of consumer purchasing behavior, and looks specifically at the relationship between penetration (number of users of a brand) and purchase frequency (how often the brand is bought).

Chapter 13 provides a list of operational lessons for advertisers.

Appendices

The six appendices contain information that illuminates and underlines the conclusions from the earlier parts of the book.

Appendix A analyzes the short-term volatility of markets, and demonstrates how it is impossible to understand the short-term and long-term effectiveness of advertising without an appreciation of this volatility—and the reasons for it.

Appendix B describes the first, pioneering, use of pure single-source research by Colin McDonald in 1966. (In Chapter 4, I compare my own research and McDonald's for their implications for media buying practice).

Appendix C reviews the progress of single-source and scanner research in the United States during the quarter-century following McDonald's initial study.

Appendix D analyzes the logic of STAS, the device used in this book to measure the short-term sales-generating effectiveness of advertising.

Appendix E describes the calculation of advertising intensity used in this book.

Appendix F lists the brands covered by this research.

Part 1

Five Discoveries

1

The Single-Source Breakthrough

This book is concerned exclusively with sales and how advertising influences them. To make this point more precisely, I believe that advertising works only when it influences consumer purchasing behavior. This does not only mean that nonbuyers must be persuaded to become first-time buyers, nor that current buyers should be persuaded to buy more of the brand than before. On the contrary, advertising can sometimes be effective if it helps maintain a brand's existing users and their buying levels. This is known technically as protecting the brand's franchise and keeping up the current levels of purchase frequency.

It can even work if sales are going down as a result of competitive pressure on the brand in the marketplace, because effective advertising may be helping to slow this process. Finally, a behavioral effect can be felt if buyers are persuaded to pay a premium price for an advertised brand, even though sales in units may not necessarily be increasing.

There is a large and well-established research industry engaged in measuring the psychological impact of advertising campaigns: their effect on brand awareness, image attributes, and advertising recall; that is, whether consumers can remember the brand name, what qualities they associate with the brand, and what features of the brand's advertising have remained in their minds. These measures are most commonly used as substitutes for sales measures, in the widespread belief that it is too difficult to measure reliably advertising's contribution to sales. I do not accept these counsels of despair. Psychological measures are very poor predictors of sales effectiveness, for reasons which I spelled out in a book published in 1986.[1] Psychological measures can help us diagnose how a campaign is

3

working once we have determined from more reliable research that it is in fact working. But that is a different story altogether.

Advertising that Works

Advertising that works in the short term is defined here as advertising that is seen by a consumer shortly before he (or more commonly she—the female homemaker) purchases a brand, and that influences the consumer's choice of that brand. The total number of consumers so influenced and the volume of merchandise purchased should be quantifiable. This is a difficult procedure, but it is not a totally impenetrable problem when tackled with the use of single-source data: the special type of research on which this book is based. In my analyses, I make the assumption that the time period during which the effective (or ineffective) advertising is exposed is seven days prior to purchase. The short-term effect of advertising is therefore brand advertising and brand buying within an average purchase interval: the period between the homemaker's last purchase, and the next one in the product field.

The actual purchase interval varies between product categories. It is every few days (sometimes even daily) for cigarettes, every week for certain food products (e.g., breakfast cereals), every two to four weeks for other grocery products (e.g., laundry detergents) and some drugstore products (e.g., toothpaste), and every few months for many drugstore products (e.g., analgesics). With goods that have short purchase intervals I have taken seven days as a reasonable approximation of their average buying interval. With the products that have a relatively extended purchase interval, I have also assumed that a short-term effect measures something felt and acted on also within a seven-day period. There is good evidence that short-term advertising effects are felt within this seven-day window. (This evidence is described in Appendix B).

In addition to its short-term effect, advertising can often also have a long-term effect. In the analyses of the long term I measure a brand's average sales over the second, third, and fourth quarters of 1991, and compare them with sales in the first quarter. My definition of long term is therefore a four- to twelve-month period (compared with one week for a short-term effect).

Advertising's influence can normally also be felt over a longer time than the four to twelve months used in this book. A brand's internal momentum (discussed in Chapter 6) can operate and grow in effectiveness over very extended periods. In this book, however, the long-term effect of advertising is manifested in the four- to twelve-month span. The advantage of looking at this defined period is that it provides a convenient decision point at which all parts of a brand's marketing mix might be evaluated.

My forty years of experience of the advertising business have taught me that the impact of effective advertising on sales is more immediate than many observers believe.[2] The periods used in this book to define the short and long term are the best alternatives.

The Meaning of Single-Source Research

This book is based on single-source research generated by the A. C. Nielsen Company. Many people responsible for brands are uncomfortable with certain types of quantitative research, because the research industry has tended not to be user-friendly. However, single-source research—despite its cost and the complications involved in implementing it—is in essence a simple technique, and its findings are easy to understand.

Single-source is not new. However, the pure method used by Nielsen is so unusual as to be almost unique. It is greatly more valuable—but also much more difficult to employ—than the diluted method, which will also be described, and which has been used fairly widely over the course of the last twenty years.

Market research is carried out in three phases. Surveys are planned, fieldwork is carried out, and the data are analyzed. Information is collected in two ways: first by monitoring, observing, or picking up data mechanically (e.g., with scanners and other types of electronic meters), and second by asking people (e.g., buyers of a product category) to provide information and opinions. The market research industry is split approximately evenly between the two systems.[3] Advertising effects can only be evaluated reliably with the use of monitoring devices. The intervention of consumers introduces too many inaccuracies and too many pieces of inexact data to produce robust conclusions.

Sales of a brand depend on many marketplace variables. The most important of these are consumer satisfaction with the functional properties of the brand in comparison with its competitors; the advertising, as the source of the brand's added values; the price, which is mainly expressed through its trade and consumer promotions; the brand's distribution and display in the retail trade; marketplace parameters, notably seasonality; and—a very important variable—the activities of competitive brands.

The major difficulty we find when evaluating the influence of advertising is determining how to isolate it. How do we untangle advertising's effect from all the other factors impinging on sales? And even if we manage to establish a clear relationship between advertising and sales, for instance between exposure of households to a brand's advertising (based on a large statistical sample of such households) and sales of the brand measured from another large group, how do we know that there is a direct cause-and-effect relationship between the two?

There is a well-known trap for the unwary. It is widely understood that in many important product categories, such as breakfast cereals, high levels of television viewing for Brand A are often associated statistically with high sales of Brand A; but high levels of television viewing for Brand B and Brand C are also often associated statistically with high sales of Brand A. It turns out that there is not much of a cause-and-effect relationship between the television viewing of advertising for A and sales of A. The real reason for this sales pattern is that both phenomena stem from a common cause—the presence of children in the household. More television is watched because of the children, leading to greater exposure to advertising for brands A, B, and C, and more products are consumed because households with children are generally larger.[4] Unless we subject the statistics to a very rigorous analysis, or unless we look at each individual household (which we do with single-source research), we shall continue to be confused by such spurious relationships.

One way the market research industry has met the challenge of such statistical confusion is by borrowing a tough mathematical technique from the econometricians, who use it for the analysis of microeconomic and macroeconomic data.

This technique takes statistics from separate and unconnected sources, for example, consumer panel or retail audit figures measuring the sales of different brands, estimates from Leading National Advertisers (LNA) of the advertising budgets and the patterns of media expenditure for those brands, plus a number of other measures. The different data sets are compared and analyzed. Taking the sales of a selected brand as the end result (known technically as the dependent variable), all the other sets of information are analyzed to determine the relative importance of each of them as causes (described technically as independent variables). This is done by the statistical device of multivariate regression, and it is often possible at the end of the calculations to construct a mathematical model that quantifies the relative importance of each of the individual influences on the sales of the brand. The role of advertising can be isolated in this way, and as a part of this process it is possible to calculate a brand's advertising elasticity, that is, the percentage by which the sales of the brand are likely to increase as the result of a 1-percent increase in advertising expenditure alone.

This type of analysis has great practical value and has been carried out on hundreds of occasions. It is very complicated, however. It requires mathematical skills of a high order. Line managers—the very people who should be using the information—are often unable to understand it. And a model is occasionally incomplete, since it can fail to explain the complete picture of a brand's sales because of missing elements the model cannot detect.

An alternative system to multivariate regression is controlled experimentation in the marketplace. Two (or more) regions are selected, and the brand is marketed in an identical way in each region, except for variations in the advertising such as changes in copy, in the amount of media money spent, or in patterns of media exposure. Controlled experiments of this type have been run extensively, but they are generally very expensive to implement, take a lot of time, and are difficult to monitor. They also often yield fuzzy and indeterminate results because the differences between the areas are often greater than the differences between the specific advertising variables being tested.

In Britain, a technique known as the Area Marketing Test Evaluation System (AMTES), which combines regional testing with econometric evaluation, was developed by Beecham (now Smith Kline Beecham) and has been used successfully for a number of years.[5] AMTES has not been employed much in the United States. Its lack of popularity here has been difficult to understand (but may be due to suspicion of any techniques developed in foreign countries!)

The general fault of the econometric systems is their mathematical complexity: the inevitable consequence of the way in which they attempt to describe a complex world. The problem with marketplace experimentation is expense, plus the practical impediments to finding comparable regions. In the face of these difficulties, the ingenuity of market researchers eventually succeeded in producing a third system that is both original and simple, and that holds the promise of replacing both econometrics and market experimentation as a device for measuring accurately advertising's contribution to sales.

This was the genesis of single-source research. The technique focuses attention on the fieldwork stage rather than the analytical stage, and it does this at the very beginning of the research by bringing together the data that must be compared to establish statistical relationships.

With single-source research, the information is collected at the same time from the same people. It brings together a household's exposure to marketing stimuli (e.g., a brand's advertising) and purchases of that brand within the same household. An experienced marketing practitioner has described this method as the missing link in consumer product research.

Single-source is however a description that has come to be interpreted imprecisely. It is now generally seen as research that can be carried out in a number of different ways and with varying degrees of rigor. In particular, the phrase "a household's exposure to marketing stimuli (e.g., a brand's advertising)" is capable of more than one meaning.

At the looser extreme, household exposure to advertising can be measured in a simple way by looking at consumer purchasing of identified brands and at these consumers' general media exposure. This is the type of information provided by Mediamark Research Inc. (MRI) and Simmons Market Research Bureau (SMRB) and used for media targeting. It represents a significant step beyond relying on demographics. At the looser end, also, are the types of single-source research that concentrate on area testing: a system by which variations in the amounts of a brand's advertising received by consumers in different regions are related to the brand's purchases by those same consumers. In this book I name systems like these *diluted single-source research*.

They are different from the method employed when the system was first explored. This exploration took place in the United Kingdom in 1966, and the person most associated with the work was Colin McDonald. (McDonald's study is described in detail in Appendix B). I call McDonald's original system *pure single-source research*.

Pure single-source research determines each household's reception of advertising for specific identified brands, and it relates this to the purchasing of those same brands by the same household shortly after the advertising.

All single-source research (pure and diluted) captures the short-term sales effect of advertising. It does this by focusing on the individual household. The data collection system is described technically as *disaggregated*, and from this disaggregated foundation—from this large collection of statistical observations, or little bits of knowledge each relating to separate homes—the figures can be clustered (or aggregated), to throw light on the variables in which we are interested. In its ability to isolate one variable while all the others remain constant, single-source research bears some resemblance to marketplace experimentation: a long-established and (despite its problems) often respected technique.

Remember that with single-source research, the different types of data are collected together within the same household. We do not need to relate the various data sets to one another after the event, at the analysis stage (as with multivariate regression), because this has already taken place at the fieldwork stage. The clusters of statistical observations simply have to be assembled in a common-sense way to throw light on the problem being examined, for example, is there any difference between the purchasing of a brand by those households that receive advertisements for it and by the households that do not?

As mentioned, the first use of pure single-source research was by Colin McDonald in the United Kingdom in 1966. During the 1970s and 1980s, new types of single-source research were introduced, and the meaning of single-source underwent some mutations, and the concept itself became diluted. The proceedings of various conferences sponsored by the Advertising Research Foundation (ARF) and devoted to this type of research use at least fourteen separate definitions, all different from that given in this chapter.[6]

During the 1980s, single-source research began to lose its focus on advertising and therefore its unique advantage: its ability to measure advertising effects. It became increasingly associated with scanner data collected at the checkout of foodstores. The term also came to mean data relating to a substantial number of variables. Indeed advertising descended in importance as promotional actions of different types began to take more prominent places in data collection (reflecting the fact that promotions were beginning to account for more of an advertiser's dollars than advertising itself). These developments are reviewed in Appendix C.

In this book, however, I go back to the origins of single-source research, and the data I publish and analyze are based on household purchasing, and are mainly concerned with the relationship between the identified advertising for specific brands and the sales of those brands. In other words, I am primarily concerned with pure single-source research, as defined in this chapter.

Repeat-Purchase Packaged Goods

This book is devoted to ongoing campaigns for established brands, although it does not exclude reintroductions and improvements, known as restages or repositionings, that take place with most brands every three or four years. Nor does it exclude launches of new brands. However, the emphasis on continuous campaigns whose budgets do not vary widely from year to year means that this book describes a different field from that examined by the study published in 1991 by Information Resources Inc. (IRI), which reviewed 293 tests of increased advertising expenditure.[7] The IRI study is discussed in Appendix C.

I am concerned in this work exclusively with repeat-purchase packaged goods, described in Britain as fast moving consumer goods or FMCG. These are mass-market, low-priced products for household consumption bought in supermarkets, food stores, drug stores, and mass merchandisers (e.g., Wal-Mart). They are sold to homemakers who are mostly, although not invariably, women. More than 15 percent of American households have a male homemaker rather than a female one. (As a broad average, Nielsen consumer panel data show that about 20 percent of household buying is done by men). What is more, men are present when a third or more of all household shopping takes place: doing the shopping alone or accompanying the lady of the house. In this book, I am nevertheless going to follow the widely established convention of referring to the average homemaker as "she" rather than "he", but readers should be aware that the man is often an important decision-maker: either as homemaker or as someone interested in household affairs.

Advertising plays a pivotal role in selling repeat-purchase packaged goods, making such products very important to the advertising business, despite the fact that they account in total for less than 40 percent of all advertising expenditure in the United States.[8] Manufacturers of these products are the most knowledgeable and sophisticated advertisers of all, with the result that we know more about advertising for repeat-purchase packaged goods than we do about that in any other field (with the exception of direct response—mainly mail-order advertising—which by its nature lends itself to precise quantification). Single-source research is employed virtually exclusively to measure the sales of brands in repeat-purchase categories.

The Measurement of Advertising Effects

In this book, advertising effects are measured by national figures specially tabulated from the Nielsen Household Panel. A full year's data have been used, although six months would have been enough in many cases. Advertisers will however be conscious that a year or even six months of national advertising is a high price to pay for confirming the effectiveness or ineffectiveness of any advertising campaign.

But any alternative to measuring the short-term sales effect of advertising produces a much worse outcome: in fact a dangerous one, because of the vast waste of media dollars that might result. In the past, ineffective campaigns have sometimes run for years, which often has meant a total waste of substantial sums of money. And in those cases when sales were maintained, nothing could be known about the reasons for the success except misleading inferences about the supposed effectiveness of the campaigns.

Pure single-source research is unique and it represents a research breakthrough. This book is an analysis of what has been discovered; it is not an attempt to sell the Nielsen system. Indeed, it is by no means certain that the Nielsen service will continue in its present form in the future; it was originally set up on a quasi-experimental basis.

Whether or not pure single-source research eventually becomes a part of the American market research scene depends on the ability of advertisers to appreciate its great value. However, it is difficult to accept that advertisers would prefer to risk wasting money on bad advertising than to spend money to discover definitively whether their advertising is bad or good.

In my opinion, a search for alternative systems that might yield equally sensitive and accurate information on the effects of advertising would be a totally futile endeavor. The American research industry managed to drill a vast number of dry holes during the quarter-century that passed between the first use of pure single-source research in the 1960s and its eventual national implementation by Nielsen in the 1990s. Further exploration will result in nothing but more dry holes. Advertisers will have to bite the bullet and pay the price for the contributions that pure single-source research can make toward improving virtually all their advertising and marketing activities.

By far the most practicable idea for exploiting pure single-source research would be to devise a system of calculating the sales effect of advertising from test market data, but this would require special household panels in a number of restricted areas, using the exceptionally rigorous data-collection systems described in this book. This would involve heavy start-up costs. But the financial balance after a time would be favorable, because of a regional rather than national media investment. I feel very strongly that this is the direction that pure single-source research should take in the future. A permanent service providing national data should follow the success of such a test-market program; the latter should of course also continue for the basic evaluation of campaigns.

2

Short-Term Advertising Strength

Short-term advertising strength (STAS) is an accurate measure of the immediate sales generated by an advertisement and because of this, we will be talking about it throughout this book. STAS varies widely by brand. This chapter gives details of the Nielsen research method and describes how STAS is calculated. It shows the range of STAS readings for the seventy-eight brands covered in this research. And it divides these brands into four groups according to the effect of advertising on those in each group.

The Nielsen Technique

Nielsen uses three streams of data that are collected within each individual household:

1. The household's purchases of brands.
2. A record in each household, based on information collected by electronic meter, of the television channels received in the home and the specific time periods during which the sets in the house are switched to each.
3. The names of the brands advertised on those television channels during those time periods.

The Household's Purchases of Brands

The size of the Nielsen Household Panel is now 40,000 homes, properly balanced in terms of geography and other demographic criteria. The data in this book are based on research carried out in 1991 and 1992, when the Nielsen Household Panel was being built

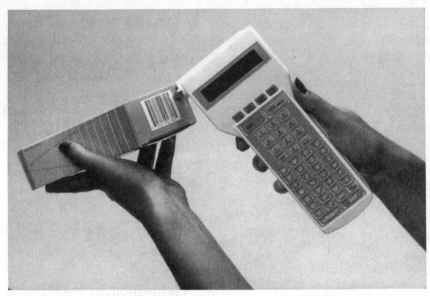

FIGURE 2–1
The scanner used by the Nielsen Household Panel.

up to its present size. However, there has always been a sharp limit to the usable size of the sample when the data are being employed strictly for single-source research. The number of homes that have the specially metered measurement of television reception is no greater than 2,000 out of the overall panel. A sample of 2,000 is an adequate basis for the conclusions described in this book. But there is a limit to the number of subgroups we can look at, because the overall sample cannot comfortably be broken down too far.

In each household, the buying information is collected with a handheld scanner, illustrated in Figure 2–1. This device is very simple to use. After each shopping trip, the scanner "reads" the Universal Product Code (UPC) information from each pack. The shopper also punches in the date, the price paid, details of any promotional offer, the name of the store (purchases from all types of stores can be recorded), and the identity of the individual shopper. The scanner has a feature that makes it usable by right-handed or left-handed people. At the end of the week, the homemaker telephones Nielsen, using a toll-free number. She then places a small transmitter built into the back of the scanner against the microphone of her telephone handpiece. She presses a button, and all the information that she fed into the scanner during the week wings its way to the computers that will tabulate it.

The Household's Reception of Identified Television Channels

The Nielsen single-source system is based (as explained) on the panel of 2,000 households with meters attached to all the television sets in the home.[1] Each meter records when the set is switched to each channel (although a record is not kept of the viewing of individual family members). Within each household, it is therefore possible to keep track of television exposure during any period—in terms of channels and times—then separate out and analyze the specific amounts of exposure that took place before any purchasing.

This mechanism provides accurate information, but it still falls short of the data collection needed for pure single-source research. For this, we must identify the brands advertised on all the different television channels in all the regions: in particular during the times when the sets in the panel households are switched on. This is a more complicated procedure altogether.

The Names of the Brands

Recording the identities of the advertised brands is the most laborious and painstaking part of the Nielsen system. The information comes from a data collection method entitled Monitor Plus, which is based on a chain of monitoring stations that keep a running log of the advertising that appears, at fifteen-second intervals, in the twenty-three largest Designated Market Areas (DMAs) in the United States. These cover 52 percent of the total population and all of Nielsen's 2,000 households used in this research. In each region, the information is collected from all the main stations, network and cable, that are watched in the region.

The technical controls over the monitoring are stringent. And there are devices—some of them extremely ingenious—to identify separately the network commercials, the commercials that appear on cable stations, the ones appearing on local stations, and those that are screened through the rather shadowy process of barter syndication.

On average, 2.5 million commercials are logged every month. Table 2–1 reproduces the report covering a small part of the data collected for the Atlanta area in February 1992. This table, which deals with only two advertisers out of the much larger number who advertised in the region, contains more than 200 separate pieces of data. Without this sort of widely collected, dense, accurate information, it would simply not be possible to carry out pure single-source research on anything like a national scale.

It is a separate problem—and one of great complexity—to extract and integrate the huge amount of information in the three data streams that originate in each household: figures on brand purchasing, on television exposure, and on the specific names advertised on the air. These three streams are all originally collected with mechanical devices, and are, within their limits, meticulously accurate.

In my work with A.C. Nielsen, the computer programs to bring the data streams together were operated (and in many cases devised) by the three talented members of the multidisciplinary team to whom this book is dedicated. I provided a menu of information I needed to test specific marketing hypotheses. My Nielsen colleagues, because of their skills and their intimate knowledge of the Nielsen databases, found ways of generating the specific information I needed, or at least serviceable approximations.

My investigation covered twelve product fields, using 1991 data but referring occasionally to 1992 sales. Although sales are volatile when monitored on a week-by-week basis, annual changes tend to be minor, so that my concentration on 1991 data will show typical patterns. My categories were chosen to be typical of the field of repeat-purchase packaged goods as a whole, and to offer a reasonable spread of products. These product groups vary in their advertising intensity and in the number of advertised brands in each. A very important point about these categories is that television is by far their most important advertising medium. This is the case for the majority of repeat-purchase packaged goods, but there are exceptions (notably cigarettes and hard liquor). Each product field was given a letter code, as shown in Table 2–2.

The third column shows the upper limit of the statistical sample: the number of purchases among the 2,000 households recorded in 1991 in each product category. In Category A for instance, the 8,385 purchases show that the average household bought the product more than four times (8,385 divided by 2,000). The subsamples

TABLE 2-1
Extract From Monitor Plus Data, from Atlanta, February 1992

PARENT/BRAND/STATION	N/L
DAY DATE COML TIME LEN PROGRAM	
BANKERS NOTE STR-APPAREL CONT'D	
*GNX CONT'D	
FR 02/07 12:19:19X 30 DENNIS MILLER SHOW	
*SB	
MO 02/03 11:26:12A 30 MAURY POVICH SHOW	
MO 02/03 06:36:53P 30 LOCAL NEWS	
TU 02/04 07:49:42A 30 GOOD MORNING AMERICA	
TU 02/04 09:56:40A 30 SALLY JESSY RAPHAEL	
WE 02/05 11:17:05A 30 MAURY POVICH SHOW	
WE 02/05 12:40:44X 30 HARD COPY	
WE 02/05 12:59:15X 30 BREAK	
TH 02/06 07:22:52A 30 GOOD MORNING AMERICA	
FR 02/07 09:35:23A 30 SALLY JESSY RAPHAEL	
FR 02/07 12:55:47X 30 BREAK	
WTBS	
MO 02/03 01:01:00P 30 PERRY MASON	
MO 02/03 07:07:04P 30 ADDAMS FAMILY	
MO 02/03 10:28:08P 30 LOCAL MOVIE	
MO 02/03 11:03:17P 30 LOCAL MOVIE	
TU 02/04 09:41:06A 30 LITTLE HOUSE ON PRAI	
TU 02/04 12:48:43P 30 PERRY MASON	
TU 02/04 06:07:09P 30 BEVERLY HILLBILLIES	
TU 02/04 09:06:48P 30 LOCAL MOVIE	
TU 02/04 09:43:04P 30 LOCAL MOVIE	
TU 02/04 12:20:16X 30 LOCAL MOVIE	
TU 02/04 12:55:18X 30 LOCAL MOVIE	
WE 02/05 11:01:24A 30 LOCAL MOVIE	
WE 02/05 05:18:26P 30 GOOD TIMES	
WE 02/05 08:22:26P 30 LOCAL MOVIE	
WE 02/05 08:59:34P 30 LOCAL MOVIE	
WE 02/05 11:23:21P 30 LOCAL MOVIE	
WE 02/05 12:16:36X 30 LOCAL MOVIE	
TH 02/06 10:30:54A 30 LOCAL MOVIE	
TH 02/06 07:32:07P 30 BREAK	
TH 02/06 10:46:21P 30 LOCAL MOVIE	
TH 02/06 11:37:43P 30 LOCAL MOVIE	
FR 02/07 12:50:47P 30 PERRY MASON	
FR 02/07 06:17:48P 30 BEVERLY HILLBILLIES	
WXIA	
TU 02/04 08:50:06A 30 TODAY SHOW	
TU 02/04 12:57:03P 30 LOCAL NEWS	
WF 02/05 05:25:50P 30 LOCAL NEWS	
TH 02/06 08:48:56A 30 TODAY SHOW	
TH 02/06 12:37:26P 30 LOCAL NEWS	
TH 02/06 06:36:43P 30 LOCAL NEWS	
FR 02/07 12:17:33P 30 LOCAL NEWS	
FR 02/07 04:59:53P 30 BREAK	
BASS BROTHERS	
GCTV CABLE TV SVCS	L
*AGA	
MO 01/27 09:16:59A 30 LIVE REGIS AND KATHI	
MO 01/27 09:27:29A 30 LIVE REGIS AND KATHI	
TU 01/28 10:35:08A 30 GERALDO	
TU 01/28 04:24:49P 30 INSIDE EDITION	
WE 01/29 09:36:26A 30 LIVE REGIS AND KATHI	
WE 01/29 04:39:13P 30 CURRENT AFFAIR	
TH 01/30 09:20:17A 30 LIVE REGIS AND KATHI	
TH 01/30 11:59:46A 30 BREAK	
FR 01/31 07:22:50A 30 CBS THIS MORNING 1	
FR 01/31 08:59:26A 30 BREAK	
FR 01/31 12:26:09P 30 LOCAL NEWS	
FR 01/31 05:53:36P 30 LOCAL NEWS	
SA 02/01 12:00:47M 30 MAGNUM P.I.-SYND	
MO 02/03 08:58:56A 30 BREAK	
MO 02/03 12:25:34P 30 LOCAL NEWS	
MO 02/03 03:23:10P 30 GUIDING LIGHT	
MO 02/03 05:21:46P 30 LOCAL NEWS	
TU 02/04 07:59:24A 30 BREAK	
TU 02/04 08:59:24A 30 BREAK	
WE 02/05 09:29:39A 30 LIVE REGIS AND KATHI	
WE 02/05 10:50:58A 30 GERALDO	
WE 02/05 12:14:32P 30 LOCAL NEWS	
WE 02/05 05:41:04P 30 LOCAL NEWS	
TH 02/06 09:18:59A 30 LIVE REGIS AND KATHI	
TH 02/06 04:55:18P 30 CURRENT AFFAIR	
TH 02/06 12:59:53X 30 BREAK	
FR 02/07 12:26:31A 30 BREAK	
FR 02/07 10:47:51A 30 GERALDO	
SA 02/08 12:41:28X 30 MAGNUM P.I.-SYND	
MO 02/10 08:58:56A 30 BREAK	
MO 02/10 04:28:57P 30 BREAK	
TU 02/11 09:56:48A 30 LIVE REGIS AND KATHI	
TU 02/11 12:19:26P 30 WINTER OLYMPICS TUE	
TU 02/11 12:29:26P 30 BREAK	
TU 02/11 04:28:57P 30 BREAK	
WE 02/12 05:53:48P 30 LOCAL NEWS	
TH 02/13 08:59:26A 30 BREAK	
TH 02/13 10:13:50A 30 GERALDO	
TH 02/13 01:29:26P 30 BREAK	
TH 02/13 12:56:49X 30 ARSENIO HALL SHOW	
FR 02/14 09:24:06A 30 LIVE REGIS AND KATHI	
FR 02/14 10:55:30A 30 GERALDO	
SA 02/15 12:37:50X 30 MAGNUM P.I.-SYND	
MO 02/17 09:14:06A 30 LIVE REGIS AND KATHI	
MO 02/17 10:48:57A 30 GERALDO	
MO 02/17 12:53:42P 30 NEWHART-SYND	
TU 02/18 08:58:23A 30 BREAK	
TU 02/18 12:21:55P 30 WINTER OLYMPICS TUE	
TU 02/18 04:17:00P 30 INSIDE EDITION	
TU 02/18 08:58:56A 30 BREAK	
WE 02/19 12:58:16P 30 YOUNG AND THE RESTLE	
TH 02/20 09:39:40A 30 LIVE REGIS AND KATHI	
TH 02/20 05:16:42P 30 LOCAL NEWS	
FR 02/21 10:33:01A 30 GERALDO	
FR 02/21 04:19:40P 30 INSIDE EDITION	
SA 02/22 12:39:47X 30 MAGNUM P.I.-SYND	
*ATL	
WE 01/29 10:36:08P 30 HUNTER-SYND	
TH 01/30 07:03:23P 30 CHEERS-SYND	
SA 02/01 05:14:14P 30 LOCAL MOVIE	
SA 02/01 07:17:37P 30 LOCAL MOVIE	
SU 02/02 06:31:31P 30 LOCAL SPECIAL	

PARENT/BRAND/STATION	N/L
DAY DATE COML TIME LEN PROGRAM	
GCTV CABLE TV SVCS CONT'D	
*ATL CONT'D	
WE 02/05 09:20:31P 30 LOCAL MOVIE	
FR 02/07 10:31:30P 30 HUNTER-SYND	
SA 02/08 11:02:09A 30 ATLANTA JAMS	
SA 02/08 06:38:51P 30 LOCAL MOVIE	
SU 02/09 11:58:10A 30 BREAK	
SU 02/09 06:15:26P 30 GROWING PAINS-SYND	
TU 02/11 09:15:55P 30 LOCAL MOVIE	
SA 02/15 04:35:28P 30 LOCAL MOVIE	
SA 02/15 07:27:07P 30 LOCAL MOVIE	
SU 02/16 06:43:59P 30 CHEERS-SYND	
TU 02/18 09:29:15P 30 LOCAL MOVIE	
WE 02/19 11:02:16P 30 MASH	
SA 02/22 11:22:31A 30 ATLANTA JAMS	
SA 02/22 06:51:42P 30 LOCAL MOVIE	
SU 02/23 02:23:04P 30 LOCAL MOVIE	
SU 02/23 06:04:38P 30 GROWING PAINS-SYND	
WGNX	
MO 01/27 09:24:19P 30 LOCAL MOVIE	
WE 01/29 10:56:41P 30 LOCAL MOVIE	
TH 01/30 09:40:34P 30 LOCAL MOVIE	
FR 01/31 05:46:34P 30 CHARLES IN CHARGE	
SA 02/01 09:52:30P 30 LOCAL MOVIE	
MO 02/03 09:13:38P 30 LOCAL MOVIE	
TU 02/04 06:02:34P 30 DIFFERENT WORLD-SYND	
TH 02/06 06:27:00P 30 BREAK	
SA 02/08 09:31:31A 30 SABAN'S LITTLE MERMA	
SA 02/08 05:10:05P 30 LOCAL MOVIE	
SU 02/09 08:31:05P 30 LOCAL MOVIE	
TH 02/13 06:27:12P 30 BREAK	
TH 02/13 08:30:18P 30 LOCAL MOVIE	
FR 02/14 05:32:25P 30 CHARLES IN CHARGE	
SA 02/15 10:21:03P 30 LOCAL NEWS	
SU 02/16 09:11:41P 30 LOCAL MOVIE	
MO 02/17 06:18:20P 30 DIFFERENT WORLD-SYND	
WE 02/19 10:21:45P 30 LOCAL NEWS	
FR 02/21 10:43:23P 30 LOCAL NEWS	
SA 02/22 10:37:52A 30 SOUL TRAIN	
SA 02/22 07:59:14P 30 BREAK	
SU 02/23 10:49:16P 30 LOCAL NEWS	
WSB	
MO 01/27 12:26:56P 30 BREAK	
TU 01/28 04:56:40P 30 OPRAH WINFREY	
WE 01/29 12:09:42P 30 LOCAL NEWS	
TH 01/30 04:56:04P 30 BREAK	
TU 02/04 12:09:37P 30 LOCAL NEWS	
WE 02/05 06:16:47P 30 LOCAL NEWS	
TH 02/06 12:12:43P 30 LOCAL NEWS	
FR 02/07 04:37:01P 30 OPRAH WINFREY	
SA 02/08 10:58:56P 30 BREAK	
SU 02/09 12:05:06X 30 G MICHAELS SPRTS MAC	
MO 02/10 10:56:30A 30 DONAHUE	
TU 02/11 05:45:21P 30 PEOPLES COURT	
WE 02/12 04:18:33P 30 OPRAH WINFREY	
TH 02/13 01:35:57P 30 ALL MY CHILDREN	
MO 02/17 05:39:50P 30 PEOPLES COURT	
TU 02/18 11:55:32A 30 MAURY POVICH SHOW	
WE 02/19 05:25:22P 30 LOCAL NEWS	
FR 02/21 12:26:50P 30 LOCAL NEWS	
FR 02/21 05:47:06P 30 PEOPLES COURT	
SA 02/22 10:59:27P 30 BREAK	
WTBS	
MO 01/27 06:07:35P 30 BEVERLY HILLBILLIES	
MO 01/27 09:44:10P 30 LOCAL MOVIE	
TU 01/28 07:06:04A 30 TOM AND JERRY CARTOO	
TU 01/28 04:38:49P 30 BRADY BUNCH	
TU 01/28 10:54:08P 30 WRESTLING	
WE 01/29 07:35:17A 30 TOM AND JERRY CARTOO	
WE 01/29 07:32:23P 30 BREAK	
WE 01/29 08:01:02P 30 SANFORD AND SON	
WE 02/05 08:07:16P 30 SANFORD AND SON	
TH 01/30 07:33:49A 30 TOM AND JERRY CARTOO	
FR 01/31 07:24:21A 30 TOM AND JERRY CARTOO	
FR 01/31 08:01:15P 30 BREAK	
FR 01/31 09:44:00P 30 LOCAL MOVIE	
SU 02/02 09:24:28P 30 NATIONAL GEOGRAPHIC	
SU 02/02 09:38:59P 30 NATIONAL GEOGRAPHIC	
WE 02/05 07:36:43A 30 TOM AND JERRY CARTOO	
WE 02/05 09:38:12P 30 LOCAL MOVIE	
WE 02/05 10:36:21P 30 LOCAL MOVIE	
TH 02/06 05:08:19M 30 GOOD TIMES	
TH 02/06 07:07:34P 30 ADDAMS FAMILY	
SA 02/08 04:19:12P 30 LOCAL MOVIE	
SA 02/08 09:45:06P 30 LOCAL MOVIE	
SU 02/09 08:02:35A 30 BREAK	
SU 02/09 05:24:26P 30 WRESTLING NETWORK	
SU 02/09 08:35:52P 30 ANDY GRIFFITH	
TU 02/11 07:06:29P 30 ADDAMS FAMILY	
WE 02/12 08:21:33A 30 I DREAM OF JEANNIE	
WE 02/12 06:16:24P 30 BEVERLY HILLBILLIES	
TH 02/13 07:44:15A 30 TOM AND JERRY CARTOO	
TH 02/13 10:50:57P 30 LOCAL MOVIE	
FR 02/14 07:41:10A 30 TOM AND JERRY CARTOO	
SA 02/15 10:57:22P 30 U.S. OLYMPIC GOLD	
SA 02/15 11:28:46P 30 U.S. OLYMPIC GOLD	
SU 02/16 07:34:39A 30 BREAK	
SU 02/16 04:03:42P 30 LOCAL MOVIE	
SU 02/16 08:42:10P 30 LOCAL MOVIE	
MO 02/17 05:23:31P 30 HAPPY DAYS AGAIN	
MO 02/17 05:49:56P 30 JEFFERSONS	
TU 02/18 07:05:19A 30 TOM AND JERRY CARTOO	
TU 02/18 07:52:13P 30 SANFORD AND SON	
TU 02/18 09:38:31P 30 LOCAL MOVIE	
TH 02/20 08:31:16A 30 BREAK	
TH 02/20 10:56:45P 30 LOCAL MOVIE	
FR 02/21 04:58:37P 30 JEFFERSONS	
SU 02/23 07:25:39A 30 TOM AND JERRY CARTOO	
SU 02/23 08:07:07P 30 LOCAL SPECIAL	
SU 02/23 10:52:18P 30 NATIONAL GEOGRAPHIC	
WXIA	
FR 01/31 10:29:07P 30 IN THE HEAT OF NIGHT	

TABLE 2–2
Categories and Sample Sizes

Code	Category	Number of Purchases
A	Packaged detergents	8,385
B	Liquid detergents	6,713
C	Bar soaps	10,562
D	Shampoos	9,361
E	Toilet tissue	11,427
F	Ice cream	9,726
G	Mayonnaise	8,094
H	Peanut butter	9,368
J	Ground coffee	8,083
K	Diet carbonated soft drinks	9,069
L	Breakfast cereals	11,320
M	Analgesics	9,032

for each brand indicate their relative importance. The largest brand in Category A has its data derived from 3,668 purchases; and the smallest brand, from 680 purchases. (The details of the subsamples for each brand do not add anything to this research and they have not been included in this book).

In each product category I concentrated on the leading brands. There are about a dozen of these in most product fields, and they go down to individual names with shares of 2 percent, and sometimes less. In each field, I have coded every brand with a second letter, for instance in packaged detergents, the brands are AA, AB, AD, and so forth. In some cases, two brands in a category share a common brand name, although the product formula is different. In these cases, a second brand with the same name as one already recorded is coded by repeating the first brand's identifying letter, such as AA and AAA, BH and BHH. In one case, there is a third identified variant; I have named this LCCC, to distinguish it from LC and LCC.

In each category, there is also a group called All Others: a bloc of small brands not separately analyzed, and aggregated into a share of market covering sales not accounted for by the named brands. These aggregations are usually under 20 percent, but they are larger for categories D, F, L, and M, which are very fragmented.

This research covers eighty advertised brands, of which full data are available for seventy-eight. Most analyses are therefore based on a total of seventy-eight advertised brands.

Short-Term Advertising Strength

Market share is traditionally based on volume sales. I therefore attempted to use volume sales as the basis of the calculation of Short-Term Advertising Strength. The intention was to isolate and compare the volume share of a brand in the households that had received television advertising for it during the seven days before purchase, and the share in the households that had not received such advertising. Nielsen found it difficult to make this precise calculation. However, they produced a more satisfactory alternative: a measure based on the share of purchase occasions. Purchase occasions are the numbers of times a brand is bought (rather than the quantity of the brand that is bought). The number of purchase occasions represents a better measure than volume sales because it focuses attention on the consumer's choice: the factor most directly influenced by advertising.

STAS is based on market share, or more precisely a brand's share of all purchase occasions. Figure 2–2 explains how it is worked out.

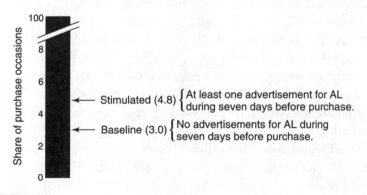

FIGURE 2–2
STAS for brand AL.

- The brand's share of all purchase occasions in the households that had received no television advertising for it during the previous seven days is the *Baseline STAS*. Other analysts might describe the Baseline STAS as the brand's natural or brand equity sales level.
- The brand's share of all purchase occasions in the households that had received at least one television advertisement for it during the previous seven days is the *Stimulated STAS*.
- The difference between the Baseline STAS and the Stimulated STAS is the *STAS Differential*.

The STAS Differential is invariably indexed, so the numbers we see represent the percentage by which the Stimulated STAS is above or below the Baseline (indexed at 100).

For each brand, the STAS measure is an average of all the weekly periods across the year. This means that with virtually all brands, a number of purchasing occasions are included. This is a procedure that gives STAS a considerable statistical solidity. Apart from this firm statistical foundation, I have also done some work to examine the logical basis of the STAS concept. This work is discussed in Appendix D.

Readers will appreciate the common-sense nature of STAS. It is a straightforward derivation of the method used in the original McDonald study, and I make no proprietary claims. A marketing consultancy in New York, the A:S Link, worked out an analytical tool similar to STAS, and successfully uses its own technique to analyze the Nielsen data purchased by commercial clients.[2]

In Figure 2–2, which is based on brand AL (a brand of Packaged Detergents), the Stimulated STAS is 60 percent above the Baseline STAS. (3.0 = 100; 4.8 = 160). This strong STAS Differential is evidence of the immediate sales effectiveness of AL's advertising. (Remember again that the STAS Differentials quoted in this book will be indexed, the Baseline STAS being 100. The indexed figure for brand AL is 160).

The STAS analysis raises three points.

First, a question: What is the cause of the STAS Differential? There are three important influences on how well an advertisement stimulates sales. First, there is the trigger itself: the advertisement, together with any promotional actions that may accompany it. In addition, there are the two factors of budgetary weight and the medium that carries the advertisements. I shall take them in reverse order.

In looking at short-term advertising effects, we can safely ignore the last factor, the medium, because the STAS calculation is confined to television advertising alone. Television is by far the most important advertising medium for the repeat-purchase packaged goods discussed in this book. This is the end result of the accumulated judgment of the vast majority of consumer goods advertisers. There is no really satisfactory media alternative to television.

I believe we can also ignore the factor of budgetary weight, for reasons that are explained in Chapter 4. To abbreviate an argument supported by much data described in that chapter, the largest immediate sales response generated by advertising comes from the first exposure. Extra weight generates very few additional sales. (It is a different matter when we are looking at the long term, as I shall make clear). For short-term sales, heavy advertising has little more effect than light advertising weight. We can therefore safely exclude from consideration any influence of the advertising budget on STAS.

We are therefore left with the first factor, the advertisement itself, together with any promotional activity taking place at the time of purchase. I shall demonstrate in Appendix D that the STAS Differential does not discriminate between deal and nondeal buying (although above-average advertising works synergistically with above-average promotions). This means that the factor that determines the size of the STAS Differential is the campaign content. This is an entirely qualitative matter. I believe that STAS is the most realistic method yet devised for evaluating the short-term sales effectiveness of an advertising idea.

The second point about the STAS Differential is that although it is primarily a measure of short-term effect, it often also has a long-term overtone. This is because a successful campaign reinforces the added values of a brand. These contribute to what I describe in this book as a brand's internal momentum, which makes a significant difference to the long-term success of many brands, particularly large ones. Internal momentum is more the result of people's experience of a brand than a result of the advertising, so that it is both inadequate and misleading to evaluate the internal momentum by measuring the recall of the advertising on its own.

My third point about STAS is a warning signal. The STAS Differential is a measure of the week-by-week *ups*—temporary sales rises—stimulated by advertising. An average brand also suffers from week-by-week *downs*—temporary sales declines, often caused by the successful STAS of competitive brands.

If we wish to protect our brand against loss of business from the STAS of competitors over the course of a year, we must reduce our vulnerability by avoiding gaps in our advertising schedule. In planning to avoid gaps, it is helpful to look at a year of effective advertising as a series of repetitions of successful short-term efforts. We need as many such repetitions as we can afford; in other words, we want the maximum possible media continuity. We should plan by the week.

As I explain in Chapter 4, most advertisers would be able to fund greater continuity than their schedules provide at present, if they were prepared to reduce the weight of their *flights*: the individual pockets of concentration within their television schedules. In Chapter 4, I discuss whether there is any danger in such a redistribution of funds.

The Range of STAS Effects

Many readers will be surprised at the magnitude of many of the STAS figures. Although these are averages for the complete year 1991, the STAS Differentials are based on individual purchases monitored on a daily basis. Since none of the brands with a high STAS Differential managed to maintain such high sales gains across the year, it is obvious that these brands also suffered from short-term losses of share. In many cases, however, the ups were more plentiful than the downs, so that where this happened, the brands managed to end up ahead at the end of the year.

It is clear from this analysis that sales can be very volatile in the short term. This was totally unknown to the marketing profession for many years. At the time when sales were monitored at two-month retail audit intervals, the short-term ups and downs canceled out, leaving relatively smooth trend lines. However, with the introduction of scanner research in the 1980s reality was revealed, and wild swings in weekly sales became strikingly evident. (This important subject is described fully in Appendix A).

I have analyzed the STAS measure for each of the seventy-eight advertised brands by ranking them in order, from the lowest STAS Differential to the highest, and then splitting them into quintiles.[3] The word *quintile* is used by statisticians to describe five groups of equal size: In this case the quintiles divide the brands according to their STAS Differential.

My intention in this research was to relate the size of a brand's STAS (a measure of its short-term advertising effect) to the progress of the brand's sales over a year (a measure of its long-term effect). My hypothesis was some sort of causal relationship, and what I found is described in Table 2–3 and Figure 2–3.

Note five important points about this analysis.

1. Overall, the advertised brands showed a 6-percent net increase in share in a year. This growth was at the expense of both the unadvertised brands and the group of All Others not tabulated individually.

2. The brands in the first, second, third, and fourth quintiles of STAS showed no net growth in sales over the course of the year. This does not mean that all brands in these quintiles were static. What really happened is that in each group (of fifteen or sixteen brands) in these four lower quintiles, the brands showing ups and those showing downs more or less balanced. This means that any long-term effect of advertising will have to be ferreted out brand by brand.

3. In the first quintile (where the range of STAS Differential was

TABLE 2–3
The Influence of STAS on Long-Term Sales

	No. of Brands	STAS Range	Average STAS	Share Growth Index (Long-Term Effect)
All brands	78	44–300	124	106
1st quintile	15	44–94	82	100
2nd quintile	16	95–106	100	99
3rd quintile	16	106–119	112	100
4th quintile	16	120–149	130	99
5th quintile	15	150–300	198	132

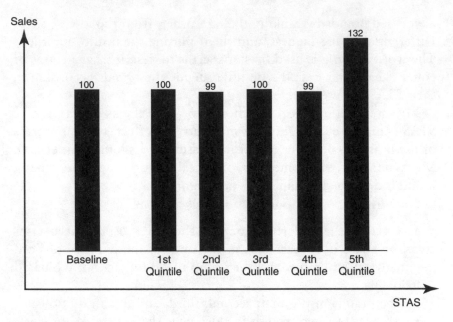

FIGURE 2–3
The influence of STAS on long-term sales.

44 to 94 compared with the Baseline index of 100), the short-term effect of advertising was apparently negative. There were fewer purchases of the brand with advertising than without it. The meaning of a weak STAS Differential is that it increases a brand's competitive vulnerability. The advertising is too weak to protect the brand from the more effective advertising of other brands in the marketplace. The advertising has no more effect than a total absence of advertising for the brand: In both cases, sales go down. It is not surprising that with a large number of brands in the bottom STAS quintile, the advertising had no positive effect in the long term.

4. The most striking feature of the analysis is the sharp sales increase associated with the fifth quintile of the STAS Differential. When this Differential reaches 150 (i.e., showing 50 percent more short-term purchases with advertising than without it), the advertising seems to kick in, either alone or more probably in cooperation with other marketing stimuli. Chapter 8 examines most of these brands in more detail, and I shall be much concerned with the other marketing forces that work synergistically with the advertising to generate a long-term effect.

5. Taking all seventy-eight brands together, the STAS Differential index demonstrates an average short-term share increase in response to advertising of 24 percent, which in turn led to an average long-term lift of 6 percent. This difference between 24 and 6 percent demonstrates the existence of countervailing forces that do not operate within the purchase interval but which begin to take hold during the course of a year. This analysis has not so far touched on the many and complicated influences on the brand in the long term. However, it does help us construct a framework for analyzing these long-range influences.

The quintile analysis will now be discontinued. I have reclustered the advertised brands into four different groups according to the effect of advertising on each. These groups are looked at in detail in Chapters 8, 9, 10, and 11, where I look for the reasons the brands in each group are either growing, stationary, or declining.

Four Groups of Brands

The basic measure used to cluster the brands into these four groups is their STAS Differential index:

Alpha Brands are those with a positive STAS Differential index, which shows a clear short-term advertising drive. As we have seen from Table 2–3 and Figure 2–3, this short-term effect has only been carried through into the long term in a proportion—a substantial minority—of all cases. We must therefore look separately at:

Alpha One Brands, with which advertising has both a short-term and a long-term effect (many brands in the top quintile in Table 2–3 and Figure 2–3); and

Alpha Two Brands, with which advertising has a short-term, but no long-term effect (many brands in the third and fourth quintiles). Alpha One brands are examined in Chapter 8; Alpha Two in Chapter 9.

Beta Brands are the large brands that appear to be in a holding pattern, and they include many in the second quintile. With these brands, advertising seems to have little short-term effect, but the brands are maintaining their position. Has their advertising been doing a defensive job? And what other marketplace variables have influenced their sales? See Chapter 10.

Gamma Brands include the majority of the brands in the bottom quintile: those on which advertising has a negative or at best a neutral influence. We shall have to dig below the surface to find out what has boosted the sales of some of these brands to such effect that we see a stable aggregate trend in the bottom quintile. What has caused the sales of some of these brands to rise—despite their advertising? We shall explore the Gamma brands in Chapter 11.

To jump ahead, there is one thing we shall not see in this book. There are no clear examples of advertising generating a long-term effect without a short-term effect first. With the Gamma brands that show any growth, we shall find that the marketing influences that boosted these brands' sales in the long term were factors other than their advertising campaigns. Advertising works. But not always. And sales are often stimulated by factors other than advertising.

3

Does Advertising Work?

Practitioners who have actually planned, written, researched, or evaluated advertising campaigns have always known that some advertisements work and others do not, and that some of the effective advertisements generate more sales than others. The problem has always been to identify which are which. This chapter provides some basic facts and explanations, based on my review of the seventy-eight brands covered in this research.

Advertising has a real but temporary short-term effect in more than two-thirds (a projected 70 percent) of cases.* It has a long-term as well as a short-term effect in less than half (a projected 46 percent) of all cases. Short-term means an immediate sales boost when the brand is advertised. As explained in Chapter 1, this is measured over a seven-day period, and the advertising effect may be lost in the next period, when the brand is not advertised. Long-term means a continuation of short-term effects, a result strong enough to be detected over a year and measured by an improvement in the brand's market share (or, with some large brands, the maintenance of its current share).

The vast literature of advertising has told us nothing until now about the overall success rate of ongoing campaigns with budgets that do not vary much from year to year. (The IRI study referred to in Chapter 1 relates to tests of increased advertising expenditure).

---

*This estimate is based on very detailed individual statistical analyses of seventy-eight brands. *Percent* means "per hundred"; and percentages calculated on the basis of totals below 100 must be projected. This is because such percentages describe proportions as if they were based on the total of 100. This statisticians' convention is used throughout this book. Projected percentages are normally reliable if the numbers on which they are based are in the 70–99 range.

Commentators without direct experience of advertising have always assumed unthinkingly that all advertising works. On the other hand, the best known estimate by marketers and experienced users of advertising was the statement made almost a century ago and attributed variously to William Hesketh Lever and John Wanamaker that "half my advertising is wasted, and the trouble is I do not know which half".

The research in this book demonstrates that Lever or Wanamaker made an accurate although slightly optimistic guess. But the really important difference between then and what we know today is that we can now establish which campaigns work and which do not.

Short-Term Effect

As explained in Chapter 2, the short-term effect of advertising is measured with the statistical device known as the STAS Differential, which is normally indexed.

The STAS Differential can be extremely powerful: doubling or even trebling sales in some cases, and therefore causing strong short-term sales ups in the brand's sales curve. But during the next week, if the brand is not then advertised, the sales can drop right down to below-average levels, as consumers now respond to the positive STAS Differential of competitive brands.

Many brands have a negative STAS Differential. This does not necessarily mean that the advertising unsells them: that it drives consumers away. More commonly it means the campaigns are so weak that the brands are unprotected from the stronger STAS effect of competitive brands. The result is short-term prolonged downs for those brands that have a weak STAS, and this eventually causes a decline in their sales trend.

Not only does a positive STAS Differential demonstrate that the advertising campaign is having a short-term effect, but it represents a screen through which a campaign has to pass before it is capable of generating a long-term effect. A long-term effect is not guaranteed, but a positive STAS Differential is a necessary condition. It should therefore be used as a gatekeeper. This means that manufacturers should not proceed further with campaigns that are shown not to have a positive STAS Differential.

Long-Term Effect

As explained, brands with a positive STAS Differential can suffer from temporary downs when they are unadvertised. But if there are few gaps in a brand's advertising schedule (i.e., if there is a high degree of media continuity), brands with a strong STAS can improve their market shares over the course of a year. In this book, I measure a brand's long-term change in sales on the basis of change in market share (to eliminate the effect of seasonality). Market share in the first quarter of 1991 is the base level (indexed as 100), and the change in share over the course of the year is measured by the average of the second, third, and fourth quarters.

The long-term effect of advertising is expressed by a repetition of the sales ups that are generated by the STAS Differential. A positive STAS Differential can lead to a market share improvement if there is sufficient media expenditure to buy a reasonably continuous schedule, which in effect protects the brand against the positive STAS of competitive brands. The importance of this point is that in many categories, a single share point can yield, at manufacturers' prices, $100 million of revenue, and sometimes more.

Along with the effect of media continuity, the internal momentum of the brand adds a further long-term drive. This momentum is partly, although not exclusively, derived from previous advertising, and its force differs by brand. As a broad generalization, large brands have a stronger internal momentum than small brands do, for the simple reason that they have a higher frequency of purchase than small brands (see Chapter 12). The internal momentum represents a scale economy of large brands, and is one of the reasons I have isolated the large brands into a separate group in this study. (They are named Beta brands).

The four groups of brands summarized at the end of Chapter 2 are composed of the following sub-totals:

1. *Alpha One*—advertising that works. Brands with a positive STAS Differential which show a market share improvement. There are twenty-six of these, representing a projected 33 percent of the total.
2. *Alpha Two*—advertising that stops working. These are brands with a positive STAS Differential which show no long-term

market share improvement. There are nineteen of these, representing a projected 24 percent of the total.

3. *Beta*—advertising that works in some cases. These are large brands (those with a 10-percent market share or more), for which advertising plays an essentially defensive role. Advertising works in ten cases (projected 13 percent); but does not work in a further ten cases (projected 13 percent).

4. *Gamma*—advertising that does not work. Any sales increases are caused by factors other than advertising. There are thirteen brands in this group, representing a projected 17 percent of the total.

The projected 70 percent of advertising that has a short-term effect is derived from Alpha One, Alpha Two, and the successful Beta brands. The projected 46 percent of advertising which has both a short- and long-term effect is derived from only the Alpha One and the successful Beta brands.

There is good evidence from the Alpha One, Alpha Two, and Beta brands about how the advertising stimuli influence sales. At the upper levels of the STAS Differential, there is an association between higher STAS Differential and higher long-term sales: presumably because of the repeat purchase that is generated by the more powerful short-term stimulus. And as a general rule covering all brands with a positive STAS Differential, greater amounts of advertising expenditure will also produce greater long-term sales. Over the period of a year, advertising provides a double drive—qualitative (i.e., from STAS) and quantitative (i.e., from media continuity): In other words, advertisers can expect results when they spend money to expose effective, creative advertising. Readers will remember the example of brand AL in Chapter 2. This showed a short-term sales improvement of 60 percent. In the long term (over the course of a year) this brand increased by 14 percent.

Advertised Versus Unadvertised Brands

The most decisive way of evaluating the overall effect of advertising is to examine the relative performance of advertised versus unadvertised brands. This research provides a large amount of information on the progress of both groups over the course of a year, and I shall examine these groups according to their consumer prices and sales growth (using data provided by Nielsen).

The price of a brand is the average of the amount paid by consumers for each purchase. This price is a product of the manufacturer's list price minus any temporary promotional offers. The most convenient and meaningful way of comparing the prices of brands, both within their category and across categories, is to compare each brand's price with the average of brands in its own category. If its average price is one-fourth higher than the overall category average, I have indexed the brand as 125.

Sales growth or decline is measured over the course of 1991, and is derived from quarterly data on market shares (to avoid seasonal influences). I have based each brand's growth or decline on its market share in the first quarter of 1991, expressed as 100. The sales increase (or decrease) over the rest of the year is measured by indexing the brand's average share over the second, third, and fourth quarters.[1] This is not a perfect way of calculating the change in sales of a brand, but it is reasonably reliable as well as being easy to calculate and understand.

The 142 brands analyzed in this book are split between advertised and unadvertised brands: Eighty (56 percent) are advertised and sixty-two (44 percent) are not. (Nielsen measured whether or not the brands were advertised). The market shares of most brands do not change very widely over time, despite their short-term volatility. However, many increase marginally in the long term, and to balance this, many others go down by a small amount. This overall balance holds for both market shares and raw sales. Product categories are generally static in absolute terms, so that the sales gains of some brands tend to be balanced by the losses of others.

In this study, I found that seventy-five brands (53 percent) gained share over the course of the year, while sixty-seven brands (47 percent) suffered a corresponding loss. One surprising finding, illustrated in Figure 3–1, is that there was almost precisely the same proportion of growing brands in the unadvertised group as among the advertised brands. This is the type of finding that might lead to earthquakes on Madison Avenue. However, and fortunately for advertising practitioners, it also demonstrates that superficial "top line" or summarized measures of the effectiveness of advertising can be more misleading than enlightening.

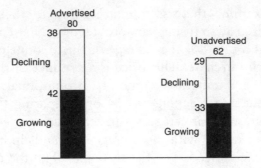

FIGURE 3–1
Growing/declining advertised/unadvertised brands.

To understand this comparison properly, we must look at four additional factors. First—as might be expected—the advertised brands are much larger. The average market share of all advertised brands is higher than that of all unadvertised brands. The average share of the rising advertised brands is 7.1 percent; that of the rising unadvertised brands is 4.8, a level one-third lower. As a general rule, brands with the larger market shares tend to be less volatile and also more profitable (in absolute and relative terms) than brands with the smaller shares. The better margins of larger brands are the result of scale economies of various types.

The second point is that the penetration of the advertised brands is much higher than that of the unadvertised ones. Over the course of 1991, the average proportion of households buying one of the advertised brands analyzed in this book was 17.2 percent; the average for the unadvertised brands was 10.1 percent (41 percent lower). For most brands, advertising drives penetration.

The third point is that the advertised brands command higher prices than the unadvertised ones. The average rising advertised brand has a price index of 106, that is, it is 6 percent above the category average. The average figure for the rising unadvertised brands is 93, or 7 percent below the category average. Another way of making the same comparison is to say that the advertised brands were priced on average 14 percent above the unadvertised (13 percentaged on 93).

One of the reasons unadvertised brands are generally priced low is that most of them have to be driven by promotions to compensate for their lack of advertising. Promotions are very expensive and tend to bite severely into a brand's profitability. It is likely that many unadvertised brands are of slightly inferior quality to the advertised ones, and their manufacturing costs could therefore be slightly lower. Unadvertised brands also save money by the very fact of being unadvertised. But even taking both these factors into account, I believe that unadvertised brands, with their lower prices, are generally less profitable to manufacturers than advertised brands, with their higher prices. Promotions take too much out of a brand's margins, which is another way of saying that larger brands benefit from scale economies.[2]

The fourth point about the advertised and unadvertised brands is that it is inadequate merely to count the numbers of growing and declining brands. We must examine the amounts by which they grew and declined. There is a modest but significant difference between the advertised and unadvertised brands, as shown in Table 3-1.

We can express the slightly better sales performance of the advertised brands by saying that on average, their sales growth was 3 percent above that of the unadvertised ones (123 percentaged on 119).

In summary, when we compare the advertised and unadvertised brands: there was the same proportion of growing unadvertised brands as growing advertised ones but the growing advertised brands were 14 percent higher in price, and likely to be more profitable. The growing advertised brands increased in volume by 3 percent more than the unadvertised brands. Thus, in value terms, the growing advertised brands were 17 percent ahead of the growing unadvertised ones (114 multiplied by 103 percent). Finally, and not least importantly, the advertised brands were larger and had a much higher household penetration. They were probably also more stable than the unadvertised ones.

TABLE 3–1
Advertised and Unadvertised Brands—Growth and Decline

	Advertised Brands Average Sales Index	Unadvertised Brands Average Sales Index
Growing brands	123	119
Declining brands	87	88

There is nothing surprising about these conclusions. But there is one thing they do not say. Advertising effects may be both durable and qualitative (e.g., affecting quality perceptions of a brand) but they are also highly selective. Advertising works very well with some brands, but not at all with others.

One important group of unadvertised brands is store brands. Nine of these are reviewed in Chapter 10. These brands as a group slightly improved their overall share over the course of the year. The special strength of store brands in the retail trade gives them a quality similar to an internal momentum, that is, they have the backing of the store whose name is associated with them. However, the consumer price of store brands was on average 29 percent below the Beta brands. To the storekeeper, although store brands may yield a higher percentage profit than manufacturers' brands, this percentage is applied to a much lower base cost. As a result, the retailer's profit for each unit of store brands will in most cases be lower than that from manufacturers' brands.

4

One Shot of
Advertising Adrenaline

The advertising business has debated for years the question of how much exposure advertising needs before it generates an effect. The received wisdom about the amount needed for a short-term effect is derived from psychological theory. This wisdom argues that a consumer must be confronted with an advertisement three times before it influences her purchasing. The Nielsen data refute this wisdom. One exposure is enough to generate strong sales.

One of the major themes that has begun to run through this book is the importance of media continuity. This strategy advocates maintaining the number of short-term sales ups for brands with a positive STAS Differential, thus keeping at bay the pressures of competitive brands whose campaigns also have a strong positive STAS Differential.

However, if media continuity is to be effective, everything depends on the minimum amount of advertising that must be shown to consumers in the intervals between purchases. How many times must the average household be exposed to the advertisement before there is any immediate effect on sales? There is obviously no point in continuously running a campaign whose weekly or monthly media weight is too low to have any influence on the consumer's decision to buy the brand.

Television campaigns are measured in Gross Rating Points (GRPs), one GRP being the equivalent of one advertising exposure to 1 percent of the television audience. Below a defined level of

GRPs—a level that varies by product category and by brand—a campaign will lack the coverage to have any measurable effect. Ideally we should start at the minimal effective weight during the periods when the brand is advertised, and then advertise as continuously as possible at this weight.

Media Objectives and Trade-Offs

When a manufacturer and his agency plan to deploy an advertising budget, they always have four specific media-related objectives in mind:

1. To maximize *reach*; the number of homes that receive the advertising at least once.
2. To boost to as high a level as possible the frequency or *concentration*; the number of times the commercials are exposed in each home.
3. To cover as large a part of the year as they can: in other words, to maximize *continuity*; or looking at continuity from the opposite point of view, to minimize the duration and number of gaps in the schedule.
4. To buy the schedule as cheaply as possible, measuring the price by the cost per thousand homes reached.

Advertising appropriations, like budgets of all kinds, are limited, sometimes severely so. This means that compromises are inevitable, and selections between alternatives have to be made on the basis of perceived priorities. This is more often than not a heavily judgmental procedure.

This chapter is concerned with the second and third of the media objectives I have listed. I have picked these two not because they are necessarily the most important ones—indeed the relative importance of the four objectives differs brand by brand—but because my research with the Nielsen single-source database has produced data that cast rather dramatic light on these two objectives. I also believe there is a sharp trade-off between concentration and continuity, and the research has thrown up an operational lesson important to advertisers which is spelled out at the end of this chapter.

Effective Frequency

The American advertising business during the 1960s began to adopt a media buying strategy known as Effective Frequency. This dictates uncompromisingly that an advertiser's first priority must be to concentrate his expenditure at the minimal level he believes necessary for effectiveness. Continuity—which becomes the second priority—depends on what the advertiser can afford, after he has boosted his weight to what he thinks is needed in the periods when he is advertising. This is the strategy that led to the pattern of television advertising employed almost universally by major American advertisers, in which a heavy weight of expenditure is concentrated into *flights* or *bursts* run at irregular intervals, with gaps in between.

The theoretical underpinning for this media strategy is that advertising is ineffective below a certain threshold level. Television is thought to have no influence on sales unless consumers see a defined weight of advertising for the brand immediately before they make a purchase in the product field. Different practitioners have different ideas about what this minimum weight should be, but most settle for three exposures. Because of the way in which television viewing is skewed toward heavy viewers, a minimum, or even an average, Effective Frequency of three exposures before purchase means that very many viewers will be exposed to larger numbers of advertisements than this.

The Effective Frequency doctrine originally emerged out of a hypothesis, based partly on theory and partly on experiments in the psychological laboratory, about how advertising is actually communicated to the human mind. This hypothesis was subsequently reinforced by an important measurement of sales effects derived from the first major application of pure single-source research by Colin McDonald.

The most widely accepted expression of the psychological theory that led to the Effective Frequency doctrine was Herbert Krugman's idea that three sequential psychological impressions are necessary for advertising to induce consumers to act. The first is to stimulate understanding, and to prompt the respondent to ask "What is it?" The second is to cause the respondent to evaluate ("What of it?") and recognition ("I've seen this before.") The third exposure reminds: a process that leads to buying (and also to disengagement from the communication—"I am no longer interested").[1]

Krugman's analysis is certainly valid for new advertising campaigns, which may take some repetition to sink in. However, most advertising employs existing and familiar campaigns. With such campaigns a single advertising exposure can be effective, since it operates exclusively and repeatedly at Krugman's third stage of reminding and prompting action. The research in this book confirms that a single exposure of an advertisement *can* be effective.

As already mentioned, the theory of Effective Frequency was subsequently supported by the survey carried out in 1966 in Britain by McDonald. (This is described in detail in Appendix B). This research concluded that a single advertising exposure has no effect on sales. McDonald's research was based on the pure single-source method. But the sample was small, indeed too small to permit McDonald to differentiate between the effective and ineffective campaigns (except for a few interesting cases of large brands, which he regrettably did not publish).

What the psychological theory and McDonald's marketplace experiment have in common is the notion of a *threshold*: a level below which advertising is apparently totally ineffective.

Response Functions

The concept of a threshold level is usually pictured in a diagram known as the S-shaped advertising response function, shown in Figure 4–1. The horizontal axis measures progressive doses of advertising immediately before purchase; these increase as we move from left to right. The vertical axis measures the sales generated by that advertising; these grow as we move upward.

Note two things about Figure 4–1. First, at the lower levels of advertising pressure—up to the bend in the curve—each extra dose of advertising generates an increasing increment of sales. Then, when we reach the bend, known as the inflection point, the pattern of response changes. Increasing doses of advertising now cause decreasing increments of sales. (In the diagrams that follow, the inflection point is marked with a cross).

The second thing to note about the S-shaped function—and this holds for response functions of other shapes as well—is that the

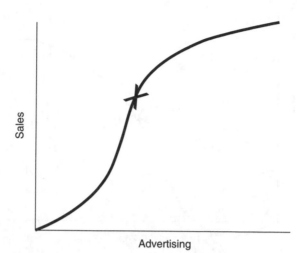

FIGURE 4–1
S-shaped response function.

data on which they are based are often soft and imprecise. The measures of progressive doses of advertising, and (especially) the measures of sales generated by that advertising, are often very imperfect, and different studies have been based on different methods of measurement. Readers are advised to treat them with caution.

The media buying policy—the flight pattern—dictated by the S-shaped response function is that at the low levels of frequency (when the sales response is growing at an increasing rate), it pays the advertiser to boost the quantity of his advertising until he hits the inflection point. This point represents the optimal frequency for a brand's advertising in the period before the consumer buys a product in the category. Frequency below the inflection point cuts off the advertising before it becomes fully effective. Above the inflection point, the extra advertising pressure generates progressively diminishing returns.

The groundbreaking McDonald study shows a slightly different response pattern, described in Figure 4–2. In the McDonald study, sales are actually depressed by the first exposure of advertising (introducing a minor inflection point). The main inflection point in Figure 4–2 is at the second exposure: the perfect level of advertising, at least according to McDonald's averages.

Besides McDonald's investigation, there are a few other pub-

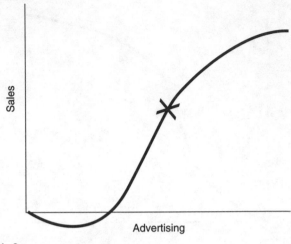

FIGURE 4–2
McDonald's response function.

lished studies that support the idea of an S-shaped response function, although the data inputs vary greatly in quality. These other studies mostly follow the shape in Figure 4–1.[2] When they were published, they naturally served to reinforce the advertising industry's increasingly firm belief in the concept of Effective Frequency.

One of the more interesting of these studies was that carried out by Laurence N. Gold. The findings of this were presented at the 1991 Conference on scanner research organized by the Advertising Research Foundation.[3] Gold used multiple regression to calculate and map the response functions for two major brands, and he showed data from twenty regions of the United States. The end product of his analysis, which yielded a number of families of response curves, was the type of S-shaped slope illustrated in Figure 4–3. At low levels of advertising exposure—below fifty Gross Rating Points—there is virtually no response to advertising. But above this level, advertising kicks in, and sales go up progressively, although at a falling rate, in other words, showing a pattern of diminishing returns.

Gold made a number of further interesting points, and I shall come back to a couple of these. But the most striking feature of his research is the very early onset of diminishing returns. The classical form of the diminishing returns curve is shown in Figure 4–4. The

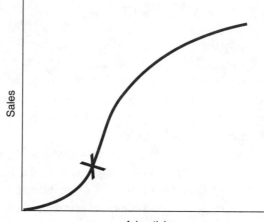

FIGURE 4–3
Gold's response function.

specific examples of response functions published in Gold's paper come very close to this. In Figure 4–4, when we boost advertising weight, moving along the horizontal axis, sales increase but at a diminishing rate from the very beginning. In other words, for the whole length of the curve, equal additional doses of advertising

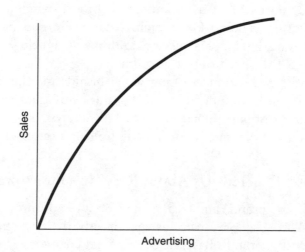

FIGURE 4–4
Response function showing diminishing returns.

pressure generate progressively diminishing increments of sales. There is no inflection point.

This curve is sometimes known as concave-downward, sometimes as convex-upward. The important thing about it is that it does not change direction. From the zero point the curve begins to lose its steepness and eventually begins to flatten: a demonstration that diminishing returns set in immediately, and operate progressively.

There are not many well-documented cases of advertising response functions of any type. Of these, however, a larger number demonstrate the concave-downward slope of diminishing returns than the S-shaped one.[4] Different patterns of response are evidence that, at least in certain circumstances, advertising performs with varying patterns of incremental effect. For example, with small brands operating in a particularly tough competitive environment, advertising effects can be much reduced, as might be expected from common sense. In Gold's words, "heavy competition depresses the overall response function."[5] I came to a substantially similar conclusion in my own review of the published cases, although I suggested that this conclusion is more complex than it appears.[6]

It is also pretty certain that differences in the specific methodology of collecting, computing, and interpreting the data contribute to variations in the shape of the response curve. For instance, McDonald has confirmed that his own characteristic type of S-shaped curve is an artifact of his analysis method (brand switching as the measure of effectiveness). He explains that if he had based his analysis on repeat buying, his curve would have been closer to that in Figure 4–4.[7] I shall return to this point.

Although the circumstances of particular brands and the research methodology can both influence the shape (or apparent shape) of the advertising response function, the STAS analysis supports the view that the most common pattern is diminishing returns.

What STAS Tells Us About Response Functions

The STAS of any brand can be calculated on an exposure-by-exposure basis. As a result, we can answer directly the key questions: Compared with a brand's Baseline STAS, what change in its market share (i.e., Stimulated STAS) is shown in households that have been exposed to one advertisement for it? and to two? and to three?

Given an appropriate sample size, the data should be strong enough for us to calculate a precise advertising response function for any brand, with the effects of incremental exposures mapped out. Since the STAS analysis is based on market share, it does not bias the findings toward either consumers who switch or who repeat their purchases. The STAS procedure avoids the problem that McDonald discovered, of concentrating on one and not the other.

The numbers of Nielsen households that receive one advertisement for different brands are large enough to form the basis of reliable STAS estimates. I am therefore going to show the Baseline STAS, the STAS produced by a single advertisement exposure, and the total STAS resulting from any number of advertisements received before purchase. This analysis provides exquisitely clear answers.

It is helpful to divide all the brands in my investigation into a continuum, from the lowest to the highest STAS, and to divide the whole range into quintiles. These data are presented in Tables 4–1 and 4–2.

The information in Table 4–1 is charted in Figures 4–5 and 4–6. Figure 4–6 separates the totals for all brands. I have isolated the totals in a separate diagram because the differences between the quintiles have some operational importance, and aggregation obscures these.

The one thing that comes very clearly out of these analyses—both from the quintiles and from the aggregation of all brands—is that the first advertising exposure has much more effect than what is added by subsequent exposures. This outcome is particularly dramatic in the top quintile, in which 95 percent of the total effect comes from the first advertisement (87 as a percentage of 92).

TABLE 4–1
The Effect of One Advertisement

	Baseline STAS	One-Exposure STAS	Total STAS
All brands	7.6	8.4	8.7
Lowest STAS quintile	6.8	5.5	5.5
Second quintile	11.2	11.4	11.1
Third quintile	10.5	11.4	11.9
Fourth quintile	5.2	5.9	6.6
Highest quintile	4.2	7.8	8.0

TABLE 4–2
The Effect of One Advertisement—Indexed

	Baseline STAS	One-exposure STAS	Total STAS
All brands	100	111	114
Lowest STAS quintile	100	81	81
Second quintile	100	102	99
Third quintile	100	109	113
Fourth quintile	100	114	128
Highest quintile	100	187	192

Note also that advertising only begins to generate a positive effect in the third quintile. In the second quintile, the first advertisement barely causes a kink in the curve. In the first quintile, the first exposure is actually negative; subsequent ones produce little or no additional effect. This negative response is caused not so much by advertising "unselling" the brand as by competitive brands with more effective campaigns taking share from brands in the bottom quintile, because the latter have ineffective campaigns. The short-term ups of more successful brands take business from the downs of the bottom-quintile brands.

In all circumstances, a single exposure in the seven days before the purchase has far greater effect than what is added by further exposures. Diminishing returns set in from the first exposure—a totally unambiguous conclusion that provides a sharp operational lesson. But before developing this point, I must make a final conjecture about the difference between the shape of McDonald's response function (Figure 4–2), and the pattern of universal diminishing returns (Figure 4–4).

McDonald Versus Jones

McDonald decided to rely on brand switching to measure the short-term effect of advertising because of his concern with the purity of his data. He felt compelled to remove all uncertainty that his numbers really measured the response to advertising and nothing else. In his view he could only do this by a longitudinal study of

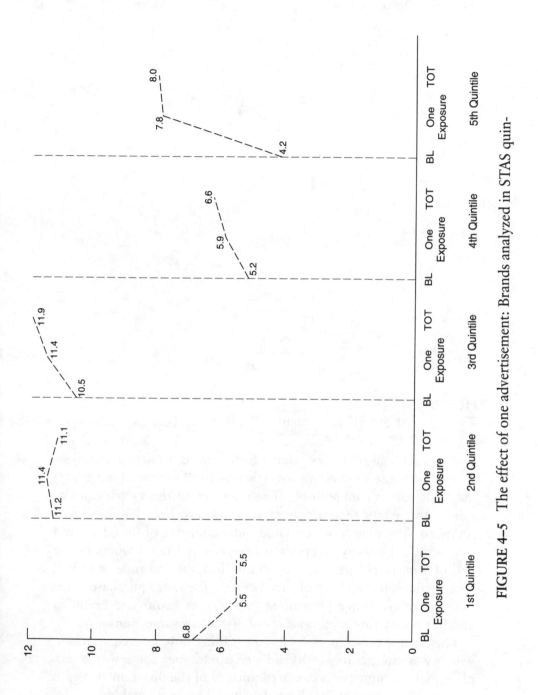

FIGURE 4-5 The effect of one advertisement: Brands analyzed in STAS quin-

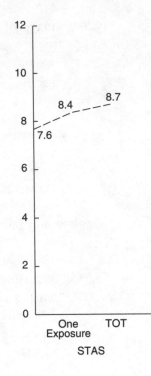

FIGURE 4–6
The effect of one advertisement: All advertised brands.

each consumer's brand switching. Switching is an active and measurable response to effective advertising—both for the brand advertised and for its competitors. "The point about the switch calculation is that every time a person switches into brand X has to be followed by a switch by the same individual out of brand X, and vice versa".[8] The only exception is a possible +1 or –1 when, by the end of a measured period, a consumer has not had time to switch back again: but the effect of this dwindles the more purchase occasions there are (since permanent 'conversion' from one brand to another is very rare, and cancels out across consumers anyway).

This matter of balance—of countervailing purchasing patterns—which was integral to McDonald's research, goes some way to explaining the symmetry between the shapes of the different curves in Figure 4–5. This point has been developed by McDonald in a carefully argued (unpublished) paper.[9]

In Figure 4–5, the brands in the lowest quintile (which show reducing sales) demonstrate a mirror image of what we see for the other brands: those for which advertising works positively. When the five curves in Figure 4–5 are amalgamated (in Figure 4–6), the large differences are flattened, although overall there is still a positive STAS with diminishing returns.

In my analysis, the brands with the entirely ineffectual advertising campaigns total only one-fifth of the whole. But if this proportion had been much greater than one-fifth, the resulting mirror image would then have had a greater overall influence on the aggregate response pattern of all brands taken together. In effect, the outcome would have been to depress the apparent influence of the first advertising exposure, and this would have resulted in a curve similar to McDonald's (Figure 4–2).

There are strong grounds for believing that the particular shape of McDonald's response function was the outcome of a large number of brands with unsuccessful advertising campaigns depressing his totals. McDonald was not able to separate his different brands because of his small sample of consumers, except in the cases of the very few brands that he was able to analyze separately, and which showed great variability in their response to advertising.[10] But McDonald's more important presentation of averaged data meant that the negative effect of the unsuccessful brands remained concealed below the surface.

If McDonald's analysis of his existing brands had been based (as mine was) on switching plus repeat purchase, the negative effect of the ineffectual campaigns would not have come through so strongly. The result would have been that his response pattern would also have shown diminishing returns. McDonald in fact made such an analysis but he did not publish it; and this result is what he actually found.[11]

From Theory to Practice

I am now returning to the decisions between alternative and equally important media objectives with which this chapter began. What does the research now tell us about the competing priorities of concentration and continuity?

The essence of my research findings on incremental advertising pressure is that, in a purchase interval, after a consumer makes one purchase in the product field and before she makes the next, it only takes a single advertisement to trigger sales. Further advertisements generate very little additional business.

In this context, I am only talking about brands that have a positive STAS Differential. But remember the mirror effect of the Gamma brands: with these, the first advertising exposure has the greatest negative influence. One exposure of an advertisement—whether or not the consumer has seen it before—can depress sales because it opens the door to superior competitive advertising.

The effectiveness of a single advertisement means that within each period of advertising exposure—ideally weekly—an advertiser only needs to buy enough GRPs to ensure that most viewers in his target group will see one of his advertisements.

This is not as simple a procedure as it might appear. It involves the construction of a family of media models for every brand based on different media patterns. It probably also means new methods of balancing the amounts of prime and off-peak time to extend reach at the expense of frequency. The problem is always to achieve a minimal reach level without at the same time boosting wasteful frequency. One media expert has proposed that, in general terms, GRP levels within the advertised period should not fall below fifty, since it is impossible to achieve satisfactory reach at lower levels than this.[12] Note the harmony with Gold's analysis, shown in Figure 4–3, which is explained by my description of his study.

The result of all this exploration will be much more efficient deployment of resources. The general media strategy today in the field of repeat-purchase packaged goods is to concentrate to levels well above an average of one exposure in each advertising flight. The frequency for most brands in the assumed purchase interval is heavy enough to ensure that members of the target group will be exposed to at least three advertisements, and in practice many people are exposed to more than three. As explained, this emphasis on concentration was the result of psychological studies published during and after the 1960s and confirmed by McDonald's 1966 research. Media buying in major agencies has hardened during the past quarter-century into rigid policies that include guidelines mandating relatively heavy concentrations of expenditure.

The price of this policy has been waste through excessive advertising pressure. And the direct opportunity cost has been plentiful gaps in advertisers' schedules because advertisers cannot afford to advertise all year. Such interruptions are a very unattractive option, because they provide opportunities for the positive STAS of competitive brands. These bring about short-term downs in a manufacturer's sales, which in turn inhibit the upward trend stimulated by the temporary ups caused by successful advertising.

This research urges a new deployment of media budgets, in the direction of continuity and away from concentration. Such a policy has (with a pejorative implication) been entitled drip-feeding. But, as Gold says in connection with one of the specific brands he analyzed, and perhaps pointing to a more general situation: "This brand's response function rewards a continuous schedule."[13] What I am proposing is a tactical deployment of advertising budgets that should be punctiliously calculated and a good deal less concentrated than is now normal.

Manufacturers and agencies should remember that if they cannot be persuaded to adopt nationally the unorthodox media strategy of drip-feed, it is often possible—and minimally expensive—to test it regionally. Most national television advertisers buy both network and spot time, and it is generally possible to adjust the pattern in specific regions to advertise continuously at enough weight to make sure everyone is reached once at weekly intervals.

In the 1970s, when I was working in J. Walter Thompson, London, the media strategy for a very large brand on which I worked was tentatively changed to drip-feed. We did this as the result of an econometric investigation that demonstrated reasonably clearly that the brand's short-term response function followed the concave-downward shape of diminishing returns. The revised strategy was at that time as unorthodox as it would be today. We therefore tested the new strategy for a year in a self-contained television region, and read the answers very carefully. At the end of the year, sales in the test region were well ahead of what they were in the rest of the country, and the advertiser and agency immediately implemented a drip-feed strategy over the whole of the United Kingdom.

When I last heard about the fortunes of the brand (in the late 1980s), this unusual but successful strategy was still being followed, and the brand was still performing well in the marketplace.

5

Advertising Versus Promotions— or Advertising *Plus* Promotions

This chapter is a study of synergy. It demonstrates that when an above-average STAS Differential, above-average advertising intensity (i.e., expenditure) and above-average promotional intensity operate together, the sales performance is greater than the sum of the parts.

One of the most striking changes in marketing practice during the 1980s and 1990s has been the continuous shift in the proportion of the aggregate expenditure on advertising and sales promotions that manufacturers moved out of advertising and into promotions. According to Donnelley Marketing, advertising's share declined massively—from 42 percent in 1978 to 25 percent in 1993.

The reasons for this trend have been extensively discussed in books, journal articles, and conferences. The most common reasons given are the cessation of growth in most product categories, which has led to a substantial boost to tactical (i.e., promotional) rather than strategic (i.e., advertising) activities; increased demand for short-term rather than long-term results; the increasing concentration, strength, and bargaining power of the retail trade; and a double difficulty of evaluation: Manufacturers have found it hard to measure the short-term sales effects of advertising and the short-term profitability (more commonly unprofitability) of promotions.

In all events, the trend is unlikely to be reversed in the medium term. Any reversal will probably depend on the eventual success of Procter & Gamble's current strategy of Everyday Low Pricing (EDLP). This much-heralded program involves reducing promotions on defined brands and at the same time significantly lowering their

51

list prices. EDLP has made some progress, although signals from the marketplace have been mixed. Procter & Gamble is persisting with this strategy, despite attempts by competitors to take business from P.&G. by promoting heavily against the latter's brands.

The relentless nature of the trend from advertising to promotions has underscored the trade-off between the two activities, and it has emphasized manufacturers' growing preference for programs that, despite their solely short-term effectiveness and hidden costs, do at least provide sales targets that can be planned and achieved, and that can be measured with reasonable precision. In contrast, the sales—or at least the sales increases—stimulated by advertising tend to be modest, not very predictable and hard to quantify.

The advantage of successful advertising over promotions lies in advertising's ability to augment sales and profit in the long term. But the long-term payout of advertising is a good deal more difficult to estimate than the short-term payout of promotions.

The pervasive nature of the trade-off between advertising and promotions has for a long time distracted marketers away from the promising possibilities of cooperation between the two types of sales stimulus. The research on which this book is based provides some surprising facts about the rewards of such cooperation. But to put this matter into perspective, I must start by looking at each of these types of activity separately.

Advertising and Promotions Operating Separately

The basic facts, derived from econometric studies and estimates of the cost structures of typical brands, can be summarized by the following three points:[1]

1. The short-term productivity of promotions, working on their own and measured by the sales increases they generate, is proportionately much greater than that of advertising working on its own. The difference in the sales yield of the two types of activity can be very high indeed. Most promotions are, in effect, price reductions, and the average percentage increase in sales to be expected from a 1-percent reduction in price is 1.8 percent. The average percentage increase in sales that is likely to follow a 1-percent increase in advertising expenditure is only 0.2 percent.

2. The cost to a manufacturer of a 1-percent reduction in price is always far greater than the cost of a 1-percent boost in advertising expenditure. The result is that the majority of promotions—three-quarters or more—are unprofitable in the short term. Successful advertising is much more likely to yield a profitable return, despite the very small sales boost that can be expected from it.

3. Promotions only very rarely produce any long-term effect. This means that there are no long-term revenues to offset the stiff short-term cost of promotions. On the other hand, successful advertising often has an additional long-term outcome to augment what is accomplished in the short term.

Advertising and Promotions Operating Together

Chapters 8 and 9 analyze forty-five Alpha brands. These all have positive STAS Differentials: Their advertising is demonstrably effective in the short term. In these two chapters, I evaluate these forty-five brands according to the effect on their sales of varying amounts of promotions and of advertising. Unlike what I discussed in the section above—promotions and advertising operating independently—the price stimulus and the advertising stimulus for the Alpha brands do not operate in isolation from each other. They operate simultaneously and in cooperation. The results (spelled out in detail in Chapter 9) are remarkable indeed.

Table 5–1 is a quintile analysis of the forty-five Alpha brands. All

TABLE 5–1
Alpha Brands—Quintile Analysis

Quintile	Long-Term Share Growth (Index)	Price (Index)	Advertising Intensity (Index)
1st	100	100	100
2nd	127	98	132
3rd	142	88	100
4th	155	81	174
5th	226	79	179

the brands are ranked from the least to the most successful according to long-term share change. The figures in the column Long-Term Share Growth are averages for each quintile, indexed on the first quintile.

The Price column shows the average price for the brands in each quintile. These are indexed on the first quintile, which represents the group with the highest prices. The Advertising Intensity column measures the average amount of advertising expenditure for the brands in each quintile (using the formula described in Appendix E). These figures are indexed on the first quintile.

As we progress from the first to the fifth quintile (i.e., as we move from the least- to the most-successful brands), we can see how this progression is associated with lower prices and with increased advertising intensity. This is what common sense would lead us to expect. However, the most interesting point is the rates of progression of the three columns.

PRICE. There is a 21-percent price decrease (from 100 to 79), associated with 126-percent share growth (from 100 to 226). These relative amounts represent a ratio of 21 to 126, or 1.0 to 6.0.

ADVERTISING. This shows a 79-percent advertising increase, associated with 126-percent share growth. These relative amounts represent a ratio of 79 to 126, or 1.0 to 1.6.

As explained, Table 5–1 describes the sales generated by promotions and advertising working together. The results of such cooperation are striking.

First, the degree of sales response to a 1.0-percent increase in promotions, in effect a price reduction, is boosted to 6.0 percent, compared with the 1.8 percent response level from price reductions working in isolation. This represents an effect more than three times as large.

Also, the degree of sales response to a 1.0-percent increase in advertising pressure is lifted to an even greater relative extent: to 1.6 percent, in comparison with the average level of 0.2 percent. This represents an effect eight times as large.

These findings offer proof of strong synergy between advertising and promotions. The outcome of advertising and promotions operating together is demonstrably—and dramatically—greater than the sum of the parts, or the sales expectation of each sales stimulus operating on its own.

The analysis of the Alpha One brands—those for which advertising generates both a short-term and long-term effect—makes the same point in a different way. In Chapter 8, I isolate and analyze separately the groups of brands that benefited from

- strong STAS Differential alone
- strong STAS Differential plus above-average advertising intensity (i.e., expenditure)
- strong STAS Differential plus below-average price (i.e., above-average promotions)
- strong STAS Differential plus above-average advertising intensity plus below-average price

I then calculate and index their average sales growth in 1991, and some revealing figures emerge. See Table 5–2.

Again there is a clear multiplication of effect. A positive STAS Differential, advertising intensity, and low price—operating together—increase the share growth to a level at least six times as high as the level stimulated by the STAS effect alone. And there is a tripling of the effect of STAS plus price.

Yet another aspect of the advertising/price relationship emerges from this research. In Chapter 8, I isolate the twelve top performing Alpha One brands: those that succeeded best in maintaining the sales impetus launched by their STAS Differential, mainly through maintaining their media continuity. I compare these brands with a group of brands that were less successful in maintaining the thrust of their STAS Differential.

TABLE 5–2

Incremental Long-Term Effects of Various Sales Stimuli (Indexed)— Alpha One Brands

Baseline	100
STAS alone	111
STAS plus advertising intensity (i.e., expenditure)	112
STAS plus low price (i.e., high promotions)	121
STAS plus advertising intensity plus low price	168

The average price of the brands with the more successful advertising was 22 percent higher than that of the brands with the less successful advertising. This remarkable finding demonstrates that demand stimulated by advertising increases not only sales but also the value of the brand in the mind of consumers, hence the higher prices they are prepared to pay. This is evidence of the internal momentum of brands expressed by improving value perceptions. Advertising clearly contributes to this effect.

In summary, we see not only that advertising and promotions can work together in strong synergy, but that the most effective advertising increases perceived value (and therefore profit) and thus reduces the need for promotions. Remember that the sales stimulus provided by promotions always succeeds in sucking profit out of a brand, despite its positive effect on short-term volume.

The strong synergy that can be generated between advertising and promotions working together points very clearly to the need to integrate the planning and execution of both types of activity: the strategy of Integrated Marketing Communications (IMC). There has been much discussion of such integration during recent years, but it is at present far from standard practice in consumer goods companies. The only one of the major American manufacturers of repeat-purchase packaged goods devoting serious attention to Integrated Marketing Communications is Philip Morris, especially its Kraft–General Foods division. However, IMC is common practice for the consumer marketing of financial products, for example, credit cards. In European packaged goods categories, Nestlé has originated a number of highly creative and successful strategies that involve an integration of various marketing efforts, and which have received wide publicity in the business press.

6

The Relation Between the Short and Long Term

The reason it is important to study the processes by which advertising works is to make it easier for the people who plan and write advertising to create effective advertisements and campaigns. This chapter explains how advertising operates in the short term and long term, and it examines how these two phases are related to each other.

Writers of advertising should be constantly reminded that all advertisements for a brand contribute to the long-term perceptions of that brand. Since these are neither necessarily nor invariably positive, creative people need to harmonize the short- and long-term outcomes of their campaigns. And executives who deploy media budgets need to appreciate the importance of media continuity in transforming a short-term effect into a long-term one.

Short-Term Effect

STAS measurements establish reliably that advertising can have an immediate and short-term influence on sales, and they quantify this effect. Advertising influences the shopper's behavior with a cognitive jolt, but one that is often communicated with subtlety and artifice. The advertising provides a reminder to consumers that they will notice and put into effect the next time they shop for a product in the category.

A single exposure—which is all that is needed for a sales effect—contains no room for persuasion, meaning the overcoming of resistant attitudes. The name and brand attributes are presented to the potential buyer in an appealing way, and that is all. There is a low top limit to what can be communicated in thirty seconds of television exposure.

The short-term advertising effect does nevertheless have some long-term overtones. The brand's internal momentum, which is a force that operates in the long term, is partly a product of what are widely understood in the advertising business as the brand's nonfunctional added values—the psychological rewards that consumers receive from using a brand. Previous advertising had much to do with building these. Current advertising in turn partially relies on these added values.

The effectiveness of a strongly positive STAS Differential can grow even stronger if advertising coincides with promotional activity. This point is made visually in Figure 6–1 by the increased thickening of the arrow, which represents the growing influence of the contribution of advertising and promotions working synergistically.

Note that I have described the outcome of the successful joint operation of advertising and promotions as a behavioral effect, and not simply sales effect. Often (although not invariably) a behavioral effect means increased sales. For large brands, it can sometimes mean the protection of existing sales in the face of competitive pressure. In rare circumstances, it can mean a deceleration of decline for brands that are faced with heavy competition in the marketplace. In the majority of cases it also leads to an increase in consumers' value perceptions—their willingness eventually (i.e., when the brand is not promoted) to pay higher prices.

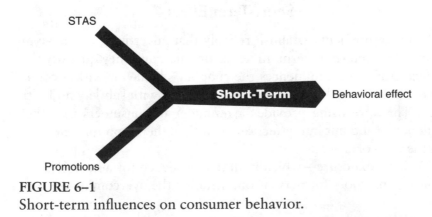

FIGURE 6–1
Short-term influences on consumer behavior.

STAS as a Gatekeeper

One of the most important conclusions from this research is the intrinsic and extended effect of advertising campaigns with a strong positive STAS Differential. Not only do such campaigns boost sales within the brand's purchase interval, but they are a precondition for long-term effectiveness.

The marketing profession has known for a long time that:

- A relatively small volume of advertising (two or three exposures) can increase short-term sales.
- Extra amounts of expenditure on advertising can progressively boost sales in the long term (although this does not happen universally).
- Progressive doses of price reduction can increase sales incrementally in the short term, and repeated price reductions can extend this effect (with progressively diminishing returns).

These three conclusions have been drawn from a wide range of cases, with campaigns of varying efficiency (measurable by widely varying STAS Differentials).

What the research in this book shows is that the effects listed above become much stronger for campaigns that have a positive STAS Differential, so that with such campaigns sales respond to a single advertising exposure in the purchase interval. This effect makes it possible to reduce advertising concentration in this interval, releasing funds to buy more continuous advertising in the brand's schedule, with the object of prolonging the effect of the campaign.

The three main marketing stimuli—the positive STAS Differential, advertising intensity, and low (promotional) pricing—work with powerful synergy. This makes it possible to boost the incremental effect of increased advertising volume by a factor of eight. This synergy can also triple the effect of low (promotional) pricing.

I must emphasize that these intensely beneficial effects are only possible for campaigns with a positive STAS Differential. It follows that since the STAS Differential acts as a screen through which a campaign must pass in order to generate a long-term effect, the measure of a brand's STAS Differential should be used as a gatekeeper to determine whether a campaign deserves to receive further financial support. Long-term effectiveness depends on the existence of a positive STAS Differential.

One of the most widely known facts of marketing practice is the low success rate of new brand introductions. The average figure often cited is 10 percent or less (i.e., a failure rate of at least 90 percent)—although this average varies according to the criterion for success used in the calculations. Pure single-source research can be used to diagnose the problems with any new brand launch. The STAS analysis will reveal whether or not the advertising campaign is effective. An estimate of advertising intensity will disclose problems of media continuity. An analysis of repeat-purchase rates will point to difficulties unrelated to advertising, such as inadequate functional performance of the brand relative to its competitors, problems of price, or imperfections in retail distribution.

Long-Term Effect

The long-term, or lagged, effect of advertising has been understood for many years by the advertising industry on an instinctive basis, and there have been a limited number of quantitative demonstrations of its existence. The most recent comes from the 1991 IRI survey (mentioned in Chapter 1), that shows that, although the lagged effect of a campaign dwindles over time, the three-year sales effect can double the one-year effect.

Two of the conclusions that emerge from my own work with single-source research are that:

1. An advertising campaign must produce a short-term effect before it can generate a long-term one. Of the seventy-eight advertised brands analyzed in this book, only seven of the Gamma brands give any evidence of a possible long-term effect without a short-term effect first. But even in these cases, the long-term effect was volatile and caused by factors other than advertising.

Some experienced analysts cannot accept that a positive short-term result is a precondition for a long-term one. They believe advertising may be working in undetectable ways, perhaps by generating a delayed or "sleeper" effect. This view is unsupported by the data in this book. I place very little faith in research used to justify the hypothesis of advertising's delayed effect (e.g., tracking studies of how well consumers recall advertising campaigns). And it is a denial of common sense that a negative STAS Differential (i.e., a short-term loss of sales to competitors) can build business in the long term, either directly or indirectly.

2. The second point is that, even with a positive STAS Differential, a long-term effect is not guaranteed. It often follows a short-term effect, but not always. In this book there are forty-five Alpha One and Alpha Two brands with a positive STAS Differential. Only twenty-six of these improved their market share in 1991.

Media Continuity

The way the long term is measured in this book is by looking at the progress of the brand's market share over the course of a year. A campaign is deemed to work in the long term if this share is boosted (or in certain cases, maintained). Given a positive STAS Differential, this long-term effect is accomplished by two factors, the first of which is media continuity. This continuity is actually the outcome of three separate elements:

1. An adequate total media budget.
2. Enough concentration of expenditure within the individual periods of media exposure to ensure that most members of the target group are exposed to the brand's advertising at least once. (The actual target coverage varies by brand).
3. A campaign that runs for most weeks of the year.

Media continuity, operating in conjunction with the positive STAS effect, leads to repetition of a brand's short-term sales ups, thus maintaining its progress, or at least its position, in the face of competitive pressures.

Internal Momentum

The second factor at work in the long term, in addition to media continuity, is a brand's internal momentum: a compound of consumers' experience of the brand and the added values built by previous advertising. There is a mutual reinforcement—a resonance—between the two, and an element of growth (unlike the stasis implied by the phrase *brand equity*). The added values are continuously boosted by further advertising, which will be noticed, since buyers are inclined to pay attention to the advertising for the brands they use (through the operation of what psychologists describe as selective perception). As the internal momentum grows, it can influence the brand's sales over periods of time that are often measured in decades.

The way in which the internal momentum works is that buyers' favorable feelings toward a brand gradually grow as a result of their use of that brand, and their viewing advertising for it, working in cooperation—but with brand use having the greater effect. When these two forces operate together, purchasers favor the brand to a growing degree, the advertising operates on increasingly receptive consumers, and it therefore yields a greater return. Previous advertising prepares the ground for current advertising, so that the lagged effect of the former is manifested in the gradually improving productivity of the latter. However, it is sometimes true that advertising can impede a brand's internal momentum although such an outcome was obviously not planned. An example would be when a campaign stresses a brand's low price, an argument that flies in the face of any attempt to improve perceptions of quality and value.

As a brand increases in size, its penetration grows at a diminishing rate. When this happens, the effect of the brand's internal momentum becomes increasingly felt in an increase in its purchase frequency (at the expense of other brands).

The notion of internal momentum is harmonious with three well-known facts about markets. First, when we compare large established brands with small brands that are not yet secure in their category, the larger ones have a higher penetration and a greater purchase frequency. People like the brands more and are inclined to use them more often.

The second fact is that, as a brand grows in market share, its advertising expenditure tends to progress upward, but at a declining rate. In other words, its advertising generates an increasing volume of sales, dollar for dollar. The campaign is effective at a relatively lower weight, because consumers do not need to be pushed so hard to buy the brand. In Chapter 13, I include a table (which I call a ready-reckoner) that suggests appropriate advertising budgets for brands of different sizes.

The third point is unrelated to advertising per se, but is an expression of the increasing esteem in which a brand is held by its consumers. I refer to the phenomenon of the most successful brands being able to command higher prices (as discussed in Chapter 5). These brands consequently need less profit-draining promotional support to maintain and boost sales.

Brands with a strong internal momentum are able to survive on smaller-than-expected advertising budgets and to command higher-than-expected prices.

Once a brand generates a certain amount of momentum, it joins the homemaker's brand repertoire, and habit plays an increasingly important role in the buying process. Consumers tend to continue in present purchasing patterns unless they are subjected to negative forces stronger than the forces driving the brand forward. The uniformity of many buying patterns, including the frequency distribution of purchases, repeat purchasing and multibrand buying, is governed by this same inertia. But as I explain in Chapter 12, this is not so much inactivity and passivity as a balance of strong but competing activity, which often results in very little net change in market shares because so many of the competing efforts cancel each other out.

The advertising-related factors that drive a brand forward in the long term are therefore more complex (and more interconnected) than the factors that provide the short-term drive. These factors are illustrated in Figure 6–2, which for an obvious reason might be called the Arrow of Effects. I reiterate the point that the short-term outcome of STAS and promotions, and the additional long-term outcome of internal momentum and media continuity, are behavioral effects. These are often measured by sales. But they can also be measured by nonsales criteria (e.g., by increasing value perceptions that justify premium prices).

The STAS effect is related to both the internal momentum and the media continuity. Taking the latter point first, media continuity is the factor that transforms a positive STAS from a short-term into a long-term effect, by maintaining the number of the brand's sales ups. The positive STAS effect is qualitative; media continuity is quantitative, and both are necessary. Media continuity extends the STAS effect.

The STAS effect is connected with a brand's internal momentum because the common element in both is the brand's added values: the psychological rewards received by the consumer for using the

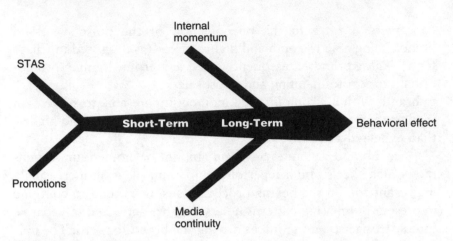

FIGURE 6–2
Short-term and long-term influences on consumer behavior: The Arrow of Effects.

brand. A creatively effective campaign—its sales effectiveness measured by the strength of its STAS Differential—is partly a reflection and partly a projection of these added values. In turn, its effectiveness—and the brand use that it manages to stimulate—generates more added values that add further to the brand's internal momentum. The internal momentum reinforces the STAS effect. The process of creating and nurturing added values is an essentially artistic endeavor.

7

An Interlude—
Successful Advertising
Campaigns

Many of the ideas raised in the first six chapters of this book will appear radical to some readers. Chapter 7 will be less so. In this, I have attempted to isolate the creative qualities of the campaigns of the Alpha One brands, based on my observation of them. These qualities are not themselves totally unexpected. Indeed, a review of the wisdom of several generations of advertising gurus shows that these qualities have been widely described and discussed in the past, although we must be selective in separating the wheat from the chaff. The voices in this chapter are not those of consumers, but of respected practitioners who made their reputations by understanding consumers.

The most important objectively measurable characteristic of the Alpha One brands is that their advertising campaigns are unusually effective. In their short- and long-term ability to generate sales, they can be judged alongside the less successful Alpha Two brands. In the strength of their short-term sales effect, they can be contrasted to many of the Beta brands and all brands in the Gamma group. Because of the importance and the relative rarity of creatively effective advertising—especially campaigns with staying power—such campaigns deserve to be discussed in some detail, despite the real problem that I am not at liberty to identify the names of the brands.

As might be expected, the Alpha One campaigns are all different from one another; the brands themselves cover a wide spectrum. But the campaigns share to a remarkable extent three characteristics. The Alpha One campaigns are intrinsically *likeable*. They are *visual* rather than verbal. And they encourage engagement by communicating their promise in terms *relevant to consumers*.

These points are more tactical than strategic: more concerned with the creative idea than with the creative objectives. Nevertheless, since a well-constructed strategy gives direction to the campaign itself, I am fairly certain that the three characteristics all originated in embryo in the brands' strategies, and were laid down before the campaigns themselves were written.

There is nothing especially original about these points, but to put them in focus, we should appreciate the features that the campaigns do not possess. The Alpha One campaigns are not hard-selling: They do not make strong and direct product claims. There are no "Slices of Life"; no men in white coats making product demonstrations; no happy families; in fact none of the most widely used—and tiresome—advertising clichés. The campaigns are not didactic and verbal. They are characterized by the relatively small number of words on their sound tracks—well below the normally agreed maximum of sixty to seventy—although this does not detract from the strength of their visual demonstrations. In general, the campaigns are concerned with consumer benefits rather than with product features. But there is a delicate balance here, which I try to describe later in this chapter.

The three distinguishing characteristics of the Alpha One campaigns are all endorsed to a greater or lesser degree by most of the best-known writers on advertising. Therefore, instead of devoting this chapter to statistics, I shall take an approach that is likely to be more interesting to readers. I shall quote the dicta of a number of the most respected experts, although I have been extremely selective in the statements I have chosen to use. The writings of these well-known people cover much more ground than the rather narrow range of aphorisms I am using in this chapter. Many of their extensively propagated and widely believed statements not quoted here will be familiar to readers: perhaps more so than the statements I have specifically selected.

Remember however that my starting point was the Alpha One campaigns. The experts I shall quote are able to illuminate the features of these in many interesting ways. Readers can however correctly infer that my omissions from the experts' published opinions were done for the good reason that my research could provide no substantiation. Perhaps not unexpectedly, we can agree that the experts are often right. But not always.

Readers will also note that I am quoting the views of experts in preference to the generalized conclusions of copytesting in theaters and in homes, and indeed any type of advertising research. My experience tells me that both the experts and the research are fallible, but I believe the experts are much less so. They are also considerably more enjoyable to read.

Intrinsically Likeable

Advertising is totally ineffective unless some people, at least, are prepared to look at it. This is one of the reasons advertising communication is such a difficult art. All viewers, listeners, and readers can recognize what advertising is, and most people turn away from it as an immediate and automatic reaction. The advertising writer's first task is therefore to think of a message compelling enough—or friendly and involving enough—to cause some consumers to pause before they switch off their mental engagement; and then to stimulate some of the people who pause to go on further.

There is no formula for doing this, but it is a striking feature of the Alpha One campaigns that the advertisers in every case manage to hold viewers' attention by giving a reward for watching. This is done by making the commercials engaging, entertaining, light-hearted, and amusing to look at. The advertisers address viewers as their equals and do not talk down to them. They respect the public's intelligence.

In some cases, the commercial is slightly incomplete, and the viewer is encouraged to take a modest step to understand what it's all about. In other cases, the commercial springs a surprise—there is something unexpected that intrigues the person looking at it. A few of these successful commercials are both incomplete and unexpected (the qualities have a natural affinity).

The commercials are often amusing, but they tend not to employ broad humor. A striking characteristic of the soundtracks of the commercials is their generally understated tone of voice. This is often slightly ironic, as if the advertiser does not take himself too seriously. This is appealing to viewers and persuades them to form a bond with the advertisers, based on the relevance of the brand and how it is presented. Music also has an important role in many cases.

The ability of a commercial to entertain is occasionally at odds with how strongly it can sell (and vice versa). A commercial is nothing more than a piece of paid-for communication with a behavioral objective. With the most effective commercials, the entertainment is embedded in the brand. If the entertainment in the commercial generates a warm glow, this is directed toward the brand; and, with the most successful campaigns, it can actually surround it.

"You can't save souls in an empty church."

—David Ogilvy[1]

"Boredom with life is so widespread a disease that I reckon the first big job we have to do in advertising is to be interesting."

—James Webb Young[2]

"Our problem is they don't even hate us. They are just bored with us. And the surest way to produce boredom is to do what everybody else is doing."

—William Bernbach[3]

"If the public is bored today—then let's blame it on the fact that it is being handed boring messages created by bored advertising people."

—Leo Burnett[4]

"You should try to charm the consumer into buying your product."

—David Ogilvy[5]

"Whether the ad made a friend or an enemy out of her before she listened to what it had to say . . . this thoroughly unreasonable and irrational initial reaction to an ad must be almost as important as what the ad actually had to say."

—Leo Burnett[6]

"We try to make our advertising 'fun to look at'—exciting to look at—but never forced, and right on the subject of the product itself. We maintain that every product has inherent drama."

—Leo Burnett[7]

"If advertising did not contain an element of reward, either in the form of information, entertainment, or some aesthetic compensation, we would be a mass of raving maniacs."

—Leo Burnett[8]

"We still don't have research that really tells us a very simple thing— Do people like or dislike an ad?"

—Leo Burnett[9]

"Yesterday's discoveries are today's commonplaces; a daringly fresh image soon becomes stale by repetition, degenerates into a cliché, and loses its emotive appeal."

—Arthur Koestler[10]

"How do you storyboard a smile? Yet the quality of that smile may make the difference between a commercial that works and one that doesn't work."

—William Bernbach[11]

"Music actually provides a measure of pleasurable entertainment. Some 'entertainment', even when irrelevant to the product, may provide a modest benefit to an advertisement."

—Alfred Politz[12]

"Advertising should be regarded as a branch of show business."

—Randall Rothenberg[13]

"Agencies are indulging in a lot of campaigns which burnish their reputations for 'creativity' but do not try to sell the product."

—David Ogilvy[14]

"Humor depends primarily on its surprise effect."

—Arthur Koestler[15]

"All patterns of creative activity are trivalent: they can enter the service of humor, discovery, or art."

—Arthur Koestler[16]

"Until 1976, Procter and Gamble eschewed music, but they are now using it, albeit in only 10 percent of their commercials. And they now use a touch of humor in some of their commercials."

—David Ogilvy[17]

"Selling consumers through humor requires a very special talent. Today, within both agency and client organizations, too much caution prevails. There are too many grim and unhappy faces."

—Amil Gargano[18]

"Advertising today serves up dramatic moments loaded with indirect sales appeals. By skillfully blending emotional and pragmatic appeals, and by camouflaging persuasion with wit and entertainment, advertisers allow consumers to draw their own conclusions about the brand and its advantages."

—David N. Martin[19]

"Advertising still downgrades the consumer's intelligence because the people who are doing the ads are often as stupid as the people they think they're talking to."

—Jerry Della Femina[20]

"Thou shalt honor thy public's intelligence."

—Leo Burnett[21]

"The consumer isn't a moron; she is your wife."

—David Ogilvy[22]

Visual

The most powerful cultural trend during the past half-century has been the development of visual literacy—the growth in communication by images and symbols. This is true of all societies, from the most educated to the least, and it is of course a direct result of the growth of television. The accompanying decline in verbal literacy is an even more important—and totally deplorable—phenomenon, but this is not the place to discuss and lament it.

Television, the main engine driving the growth of visual communication, is also the main medium for packaged goods advertising. Advertisers would be acting against their self-interest if they did not exploit television's potential, in particular its power to demonstrate, and its ability to generate mood and emotion. The Alpha One campaigns are models in this regard. And the views of our experts are, as usual, illuminating.

(From a speech delivered at a professional conference) "Everything we have done today has been in the language of words. And our market out there for most of the products that most all of us sell involves talking to people for whom words are really going out of style."

—William M. Backer[23]

"I sometimes think that a good commercial should only have two words in the beginning that said simply, 'Watch this.'"

—David Ogilvy[24]

"We can all point to many cases where the image is remembered long after the words are forgotten."

—Leo Burnett[25]

"Demonstrations don't have to be dull. To demonstrate how strong paper-board can be, International Paper spanned a canyon with a bridge made of paper-board—and then drove a heavy truck over it."

—David Ogilvy[26]

(An advertisement) "can project a unique selling proposition (USP) without using any words whatsoever. Johnson & Johnson ran a superb advertisement which showed an egg, stuck to a Band-Aid, immersed in a clear glass vessel of boiling water."

—Rosser Reeves[27]

(For food advertising) "Build your advertisement around appetite appeal. The larger your food illustration, the more appetite appeal."

—David Ogilvy[28]

"I now know that in television you must make your pictures tell the story. Try running your commercial with the sound turned off; if it doesn't sell without sound, it is useless."

—David Ogilvy[29]

"There is another gambit available which can move mountains: emotion and mood. Most commercials slide off (the viewer's) memory like water off a duck's back. For this reason you should give your commercials a touch of singularity, a burr that will make them stick in the viewer's mind. But be very careful how you do this; the viewer is apt to remember your burr but forget your selling promise."

—David Ogilvy[30]

"A look or a take from an actor or actress can often register consumer satisfaction better than any words can."

—Alvin Hampel[31]

"The ability to travel from place to place is the purpose served by an automobile. Is this a sales point? No, it is not. Safety provided by an automobile is not its main purpose. Is it nevertheless a sales point? No, it is not. The look of an automobile is not its main purpose, but it is a sales point."

—Alfred Politz[32]

Communicating Their Promise in Terms Relevant to Consumers

Consumers buy brands for the benefits that those brands give them. But a manufacturer should not believe that in a highly competitive world success will result if he only communicates a bald functional advantage, even if his brand is the only one to offer it. Functional benefits are very important, but advertising claims about these are processed in two ways in the consumer's psyche.

First, a functional advantage is often broadened in the consumer's mind into something much more emotional. This has a stronger effect than functional claims on their own, and the resulting amalgam is unique to the brand. The manufacturer's prospects are improved to the extent that this happens. A statement in an advertisement for a food brand that it has no cholesterol or sugar or salt releases a torrent of emotional signals about health and long life. The click of a camera shutter in a commercial can be transformed in the viewer's mind into a highly charged message: this click records—and in effect freezes—the high points in his or her life.

The second way in which claims are processed is that the functional (or the functional-*cum*-emotional) qualities of a brand are perceived as having value to the consumer solely to the extent that they relate to her day-to-day life. Unless a brand has functional features superior to the competition in at least some respects, it will not be bought repeatedly. But these alone are not enough. The consumer must find the brand's functional features more relevant than the advantages offered by any competitive brands she may be considering at the time.

It follows that unless the consumer is shown a brand's qualities in highly personal and relevant terms, it will have no appeal. Advertisers do this by studying their buyers. The positioning of their brands (determining where their brands fit into a competitive marketplace), and the creative idea, are both the direct result of the advertiser's knowledge of his consumers.

One rather obvious point is that advertising that shows people is likely to be more successful than advertising that does not. Qualitative research has shown that advertising about products on their own can generate cold, impersonal image associations.

The positioning of the brand in relation to its competitors must be thought out with agonizing precision. This positioning embraces both the brand's functional and its nonfunctional features. When CD—an important brand of which I have first-hand knowledge— was first introduced, its selected positioning was the end product of an extraordinary process of experimentation. This involved writing and testing nineteen alternative positionings, which were tested in the form of more-or-less finished films. The cost of this film production was many millions of dollars; and perhaps more seriously, the procedure took more than two years. But the result repaid the cost and trouble, because the brand was and is a triumph in the marketplace. It is no coincidence that it has one of the highest STAS Differentials measured by Nielsen.

An even more important point about functional features is that advertising that sells them successfully must be based on an idea. As I have already implied, this idea can be—and generally is—enclosed in an emotional envelope. But if the idea is going to work at all, this envelope must contain something important to the consumer. The commercials should be likeable—but the selling message must be unmistakable.

In successful campaigns, the rational features of the brand are almost invariably demonstrated. The purpose of this is partly to provide a rational selling argument. Just as commonly, it is aimed at providing the consumer with a postpurchase rationalization: a justification for a preference that may have been totally nonrational. Psychologists have a name for this curious effect; they call it the Reduction of Cognitive Dissonance.

"After studying just why (a magazine publisher) is so successful we have come to the conclusion that it all rests on just one thing: He doesn't sell space; he sells ideas."

—James Webb Young[33]

"I doubt if more than one campaign in a hundred contains a big idea. I am supposed to be one of the more fertile inventors of big ideas, but in my long career as a copywriter I have not had more than twenty, if that."

—David Ogilvy[34]

"The advertisement may have said five, ten, or fifteen things, but the consumer will tend to pick out just one, or else, in a fumbling, confused way, he tries to fuse them together into a concept of his own."

—Rosser Reeves[35]

"Ads are planned and written with some utterly wrong conception. They are written to please the seller. The interests of the buyer are forgotten."

—Claude C. Hopkins[36]

"You can attain a temporary share of market with a new product or a smart promotion, but to enjoy a really healthy share of market (in three years) you have to start now, to build a share of mind."

—Leo Burnett[37]

"I agree with Roy Whittier who once said, 'Too many advertisements spend so much time telling why the product is best that they fail to tell why it's good.'"

—Leo Burnett[38]

"If a product has features worth paying money for, it must have features worth paying attention to."

—Alfred Politz[39]

"We start with people."

—Alfred Politz[40]

"Reasoning and emotion are not opposite to one another, any more than temperature and size in the physical world are opposites. Both reasoning and emotion are genuine reactions. They are distinctly different, and yet they influence each other."

—Alfred Politz[41]

"The key is to find out which button you can press on every person that makes him want to buy your product over another product. What's the emotional thing that affects people?"

—Jerry Della Femina[42]

"Researchers have not yet found a way to quantify the effectiveness of emotion, but I have come to believe that commercials with a large content of nostalgia, charm, and even sentimentality can be enormously effective. . . . I hasten to add that consumers also need a rational excuse to justify their emotional decisions."

—David Ogilvy[43]

"I am astonished to find how many manufacturers, on both sides of the Atlantic, still believe that women can be persuaded by logic and argument to buy one brand in preference to another. The greater the similarity between products, the less part reason plays in brand selection."

—David Ogilvy[44]

"A better way may be found through the use of advertising to add a subjective value to the tangible values of the product. For subjective values are no less real than the tangible ones."

—James Webb Young[45]

"Most people and propositions have their natural limitations. These are inherent in personality and temperament if in nothing else. Advertising which keys a proposition to a certain kind of person may be highly successful as long as it stays true to type. When it tries to be all things to all men it endangers the personality it has established and makes an appeal to nobody."

—James Webb Young[46]

"Promise, large promise is the soul of an advertisement."

—Samuel Johnson[47]

Part 2

Evidence for Part 1—
Seventy-Eight Brands
Dissected

8

Advertising that Works: The Alpha One Brands

Chapters 8, 9, 10, and 11 should be read as a coordinated sequence. Each is devoted to one of the groups of brands described at the end of Chapter 2. The purpose of analyzing these groups is that they provide the supporting evidence on which the conclusions in Part 1 are based.

To help the reader, I shall repeat two definitions used in Part 1. *Sales Growth* (or decline) is based on Nielsen data measuring the brand's market share in the first quarter of 1991, indexed as 100. The average share for the second, third, and fourth quarters has an index number calculated to compare it with the first quarter's figure. *STAS Differential* index is the Stimulated STAS for each brand, indexed on its Baseline STAS, which is measured as 100.

Three important variables, all controlled by the marketer, have a direct influence on sales. They are a brand's advertising intensity, price index, and promotional intensity.

Advertising Intensity is represented by the brand's share of total advertising in its category (i.e., share of voice), divided by its share of market. This produces an estimate of the percentage points of advertising voice for each percentage point of a brand's market share. In this way, we can compare brands of different sizes according to their relative investment in advertising. The calculation is explained in more detail in Appendix E; the measure of share of voice is based on Nielsen data.

Although Chapter 4 demonstrates that a brand's advertising budget has little influence within the purchase interval so long as most consumers are exposed to at least one advertisement for the brand, it is a different matter when we are looking at more extended periods. Over a year, the continuity of a schedule is important, because continuous advertising reduces the number of sales downs over the twelve months. Continuity is a question of the advertising budget, measured here as advertising intensity.

Price Index is a measure of the average price paid by consumers for the brand, compared with the average price in the category (indexed as 100).

Promotional Intensity is measured by the percentage of the brand's volume sold on deal (at a special, reduced price), compared with the category average (indexed as 100). A brand's promotional intensity is related to its price index, but the two are not the same. The price is the brand's list price less all the promotional allowances made to the consumer. The total amount of such allowances is measured by the index of promotional intensity, and this index signals the importance of the brand's short-term price reductions as a tactical selling tool.

Note that the price index and promotional intensity are expressions of consumer promotions, intended to pull the merchandise through the retail pipeline. The analysis does not cover trade promotions, which are mainly financial incentives to the retail trade aimed at pushing the goods through the pipeline to the consumer. Even though this activity is not measured in my calculations, I do not imply that trade promotions have no influence on consumer sales. Trade promotions are often partially passed to the consumer in the form of retail price reductions, which are of course covered in this analysis. (A common example is when stores double the value of manufacturers' coupons).

In Table 8–1, I make four separate quintile analyses, based in turn on the STAS Differential, advertising intensity, price index, and promotional intensity (I call these the four marketing inputs, or stimuli). For each of these four measures, I rank the brands, from the lowest to the highest, and divide them into quintiles. I give an average figure for each quintile, plus a total for all the quintiles together. This set of analyses is what we see in the vertical columns of Table 8–1 (e.g., in the STAS Differential analysis, the average Differential in the first quintile is 82; in the second, it is 100, etc.) The left-hand column describes the number of brands in each quintile; the second, third, fourth, and fifth columns are each devoted to a separate quintile analysis.

In Table 8–2, I introduce another measure: the average sales growth or decline in each of the individual quintiles and in the totals. This analysis makes it possible in each quintile to compare the strength of the marketing input (Table 8–1) and the resultant long-term sales growth/decline (Table 8–2).

Figure 8–1 picks out the strongest growth quintile in each of the four analyses in Table 8–2. These are the fifth quintile for STAS Differential, advertising intensity, and promotional intensity; and the first quintile for the price index (sales being stimulated by low prices).

Table 8–2 and Figure 8–1 show some remarkable relationships. There is an astonishing consistency in the degree of sales response in all four of the most effective quintiles. The average sales increase in the top quintile measured by STAS—reflecting the quality of the advertising campaign—is 32 percent. Measured by advertising intensity—the size of the advertising budget—it is also 32 percent. Measured by the price index, it is 33 percent; and by the promotional index (related, as explained, to the price index) it is 20 percent.

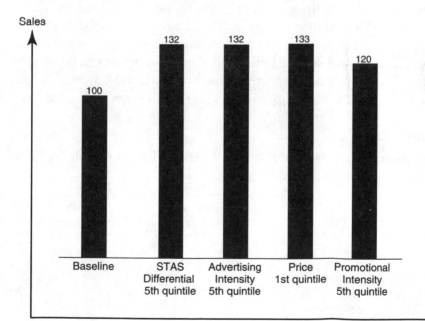

FIGURE 8–1
Top-ranking quintiles: Share growth index.

TABLE 8–1

Composition of Each Quintile in Four Independent Quintile Analyses, Plus Average Figures

	No. of Brands	STAS Differential (Index)	Advertising Intensity (% Points)	Price (Index)	Promotional Intensity (Index)
Total	78	124	2.3	110	110
1st Quintile	15	82	0.6	74	81
2nd Quintile	16	100	1.2	96	96
3rd Quintile	16	112	1.8	118	107
4th Quintile	16	130	2.5	123	120
5th Quintile	15	198	5.5	143	145

If the composition of the top quintile were the same for each of the four stimuli—in other words if the quintiles were made up of the same brands—then we could infer that the quality of the advertising campaign, the advertising budget and the brand's relative price are all equally important in determining a brand's share growth over the course of a year. But we cannot go as far as that.

The reason is that the composition of each of the most effective quintiles is to some extent different. Each comprises fifteen or sixteen brands, but not always the same brands. In fact, a count of all the brands in the four top quintiles gives us a gross total of thirty-

TABLE 8–2

Long-Term Share Growth/Decline Index in Each Quintile in Four Independent Quintile Analyses

	STAS Differential	Advertising Intensity	Price Index	Promotional Intensity
Total	106	106	106	106
1st Quintile	100	99	133	102
2nd Quintile	99	103	104	98
3rd Quintile	100	97	95	101
4th Quintile	99	100	99	109
5th Quintile	132	132	101	120

TABLE 8–3
Composition of the Four Groups of Brands

	Number	Percent
Total	78	(100)
Alpha One	26	(33)
Alpha Two	19	(24)
Beta	20	(26)
Gamma	13	(17)

two. Each of these brands appears twice on average (16 brands per quintile x 2 = 32), which means that most of the most successful brands receive a double marketing drive.

A quintile analysis divides a series of brands into units of one-fifth, according to some defined criterion. Although the brands with the highest growth appear in the top quintile by any of the quintile measures, there are some brands that show at least some growth in the other quintiles as well (although there are of course fewer such brands in the fourth quintile and fewer still in the lower ones).

The numbers of brands in each of the four categories discussed in Chapters 8, 9, 10, and 11 respectively are shown in Table 8–3. I have followed the normal statistical convention of putting the percentages in parentheses to warn readers that they are calculated from a total of only seventy-eight brands. As explained in Chapter 3, the percentages represent a statistical projection, which would not be the case if the total were 100 or more.

From now on, each group of brands will be treated separately, starting with Alpha One. These are the majority of the brands with both a positive STAS Differential and long-term market share growth over the course of one year. A small number of large brands, those in the Beta group, also had these characteristics.

The Alpha One Brands

Table 8–4 shows the composition of the Alpha One group. The starting point for this analysis was two measures of marketplace success, STAS and share growth, and the brands are ranked by the latter. Share growth is not itself a marketing input, but an outcome.

However, from a comparison of this and the four marketing stimuli, we should be able to infer what has caused the share growth if we look at the variables closely enough.

The most obvious features of Table 8–4 are that the STAS Differential varies but is quite pronounced in most cases; advertising investments are skewed, with only eight brands spending more than the average ratio; and price is a more general marketing stimulus, with fifteen brands being priced below the mean. A related point is the fairly general prevalence of promotions, with fourteen brands having above-average promotional ratios. The data in the table also contain some more subtle points.

The share growth index is described technically as a dependent variable. The four marketing stimuli are independent variables, and I am concerned with the influence of each of these on the dependent one. (As explained earlier, the price index and promotional intensity index are not independent of one another, although the degree of dependence of share growth on either or both of them is something we can look at).

If we run down each column of figures in Table 8–4, there seems to be no close relationship between any one of the independent variables and the dependent one. But connecting relationships exist, and to uncover them we have to do some averaging. Note that when we relate the four marketing variables to the outcome, the share growth index, we are looking at the combined effect of short- and long-term stimuli. (I later show a way of separating these effects).

In looking at the relative importance of the four stimuli, I have analyzed the data in three ways, with the following objectives: To establish how different intensities of each of the four marketing inputs influence share growth; To measure any synergy between the various marketing stimuli; and To isolate the stimuli that best explain the varying amounts of share growth for different brands.

Different Intensities of the Four Marketing Stimuli

A total of twenty-six brands is too small to break into quintiles. However, I am comfortable about dividing the total into two groups for each of the marketing inputs: the brands that receive above-average and those that receive below-average amounts of

TABLE 8–4
Alpha One Brands

Brand	Market Share 1st Qtr. '91 (% Points)	Long-Term Share Growth (Index)	STAS Diff. (Index)	Adv. Int. (% Points)	Price (Index)	Prom. Int. (Index)
LF	2.7	100	120	2.6	110	91
JC	8.2	100	167	0.9	101	146
LCC	2.7	103	157	2.6	130	108
DD	8.0	105	108	2.0	157	94
AK	3.4	106	181	1.2	66	116
LC	4.0	107	100	2.0	91	107
LJ	1.5	107	100	3.3	88	131
AE	5.4	107	119	2.2	105	118
BD	6.2	108	153	0.5	95	139
CH	4.2	109	121	2.4	143	94
DH	2.9	110	156	2.8	75	121
LD	3.2	112	111	2.5	84	119
MG	2.1	114	147	7.1	130	85
AL	2.9	114	160	3.4	73	128
BP	3.8	118	149	1.9	90	64
KD	3.1	119	106	5.2	87	100
EE	6.1	120	204	1.0	94	115
KG	1.9	121	142	2.7	113	83
LG	2.3	122	121	2.2	127	70
LCCC	1.3	123	119	4.6	123	123
BR	2.0	125	133	5.0	109	108
KH	1.5	127	106	0.4	75	90
AJ	2.4	158	232	1.2	81	123
CD	5.0	178	193	2.0	82	122
AH	2.6	219	253	3.5	97	163
CN	1.0	330	151	9.0	46	159
Aver.	3.5	129	147	2.9	99	112

TABLE 8–5

Share Growth from Different Amounts of Marketing Stimuli

	Total		Above-Average Input		Below-Average Input	
	No. of Brands	Average Long-Term Share Growth Index	No. of Brands	Average Long-Term Share Growth Index	No. of Brands	Average Long-Term Share Growth Index
STAS Differential	26	129	13	144	13	114
Advertising Intensity	26	129	8	155	18	117
Price	26	129	11	112	15	142
Promotional Intensity	26	129	14	142	12	114

each stimulus. The results, measured by share growth, are seen in Table 8–5.

Two things can be inferred from Table 8–5. First, as already noted, advertisers made a greater commitment to price-oriented activities than to advertising activities: There are fifteen brands driven by low price and fourteen by high promotions, compared with thirteen brands with a strong STAS Differential and only eight with a high advertising investment. These brand numbers are not an accident, but represent management choices. Except in the cases of high STAS, the numbers of brands driven by the other marketing inputs represent decisions on the part of manufacturing companies: decisions that tend to favor price stimuli more strongly than advertising stimuli.

The second inference from the table is that although above-average amounts of all the stimuli work well, the advertising-related activities (+44 and +55) work just as strongly as—and perhaps more strongly than—the price-related activities (+42 and +42). Some readers may find this surprising in view of the general rule that promotions generate more immediate sales than advertising. However, Table 8–5 is analyzing a long-term sales response, not a short-term one.

Synergy Between the Marketing Stimuli

Readers will remember from the quintile analysis earlier in this chapter the overlap between the four marketing stimuli. Virtually all the Alpha One brands are driven by two stimuli, and a few are driven by three. The combined effect of these on share growth is seen in Table 8–6. In this table, promotional intensity has been omitted because of its overlap with price.

This table isolates the brands that received above-average amounts of the two remaining marketing stimuli—advertising intensity and price reduction—on top of a positive STAS effect. Advertising intensity was measured by whether the brand's intensity is above the average for all brands of the same market share (based on Table 13–1). Brands with a price index of less than 100 were selected because their prices are below their category averages (therefore offering a greater-than-average price incentive).

Despite the small subsamples on which Table 8–6 is based, four conclusions emerge.

1. For the Alpha One brands, the STAS effect alone (with below-average amounts of the other sales stimuli) produces a lift of 32

TABLE 8–6
Share Growth from Different Combinations of Marketing Stimuli

	No. of Brands	Average STAS Differential	Average Long-Term Share Growth Index
Baseline		100	100
STAS Differential alone	7	132	111
STAS Differential and Advertising Intensity	5	126	112
STAS Differential and Price	7	162	121
STAS Differential and Advertising Intensity and Price	7	160	168

percent in share within the purchase interval, and 11 percent over the course of the year.

2. The addition of above-average advertising intensity adds nothing to the STAS effect.

3. Adding the above-average price stimulus to the STAS effect doubles the short-term effect. This can be explained by advertising that triggers consumers to buy promoted merchandise. The long-term effect is also doubled from the level stimulated by STAS alone.

4. Adding the above-average price stimulus and above-average advertising intensity to the effect of the STAS Differential causes no further short-term lift beyond that stimulated by price, but it causes a powerful synergy in the long term. The increase in share over a year is six times higher than the STAS effect alone. This increase underscores the value of integrated planning of all marketing activities.

The Stimuli that Best Explain Share Growth

The best way to isolate the stimuli that most closely explain share growth is to start with the dependent variable—share growth itself—and to group the twenty-six brands according to the amounts by which they each increased. We can then compare these families of brands with the sales stimuli (the amounts of which vary for each group of brands). The sample is not large enough to employ a quintile analysis. But I can use terciles, an analysis that isolates three groups of brands: The nine brands with the lowest share growth, the nine brands with the highest share growth, and the eight brands in between.

The important point about this analysis is that it can detect the varying quantities of the different marketing inputs that have influenced the marketplace success of the separate groups of brands, that is, what degree of advertising intensity is associated with the least successful brands, and what degree is associated with the most successful ones?

Table 8–7 shows the results, and Table 8–8 indexes the same figures.

Comparing the tercile analysis of share growth with those for the

TABLE 8–7
Alpha One Brands—in Terciles

Tercile	Long-Term Share Growth (Index)	STAS Differential (Index)	Advertising Intensity (% Points)	Price (Index)	Promotional Intensity (Index)
Bottom nine brands	105	134	1.9	105	117
Middle eight brands	115	144	3.3	97	103
Top nine brands	167	161	3.4	95	116
All brands	129	147	2.9	99	112

four marketing stimuli, we see some sort of relationship for STAS Differential, advertising intensity, and price (remembering that the price relationship is reciprocal). There is however no relationship at all with promotional intensity. And the only measure that indicates the rather large scope of the share growth is advertising intensity. (Advertising intensity growth of 79 percent; share growth of 59 percent). The STAS Differential and price measures show much smaller numbers.

We have already seen (in Table 8–5) that both of the advertising-

TABLE 8–8
Alpha One Brands—Tercile Index

Tercile	Long-Term Share Growth	STAS Differential	Advertising Intensity	Price	Promotional Intensity
Bottom nine brands	100	100	100	100	100
Middle eight brands	110	107	174	92	88
Top nine brands	159	120	179	90	99

related inputs produce long-term share growth at least as large as—and perhaps larger than—the price-related stimuli. We now also see that advertising intensity is more correlated with share growth than are any of the other measures. This means that advertising intensity more directly predicts share growth than any of the other variables.

The lack of correlation between promotional intensity and share growth is evidence of the weak long-term effect of promotions. Promotions have a powerful short-term influence on the sales of most brands, but this effect does not hold over the course of a year, because of the effects of promotions for competitive brands. On the other hand, the short-term effect of advertising is more likely to lead to a long-term effect, by the process described in Chapter 6.

There are some further aspects of Tables 8–7 and 8–8 revealed in Chapter 9, when I introduce data relating to the Alpha Two brands.

STAS and Market Share

One of the most puzzling features of the research in this book is the disparity between a brand's STAS and its market share. They both measure essentially the same thing, and the only difference is that STAS is a strictly short-term measure—share of purchases within the purchase interval—whereas market share covers a much longer period. Table 8–9 shows the STAS and share figures for the Alpha One brands. The achieved market share represents the average for the second, third, and fourth quarters of 1991.

Note that we are now looking at a trio of market share measures (and in this book the word *trio* will be used to describe them): the Baseline STAS, representing the average, unstimulated share level; the Stimulated STAS, representing the short-term effect of the campaign idea; and the achieved market share, representing the combined effect of the short-term STAS stimulus and the three other marketing stimuli, minus the countervailing influence of competitors' marketing activities. This combined effect represents a long-term outcome.

The averages of the three measures for all twenty-six brands in Table 8–9 are shown in Figure 8–2.

TABLE 8–9
Alpha One Brands—Trio of Market Share Measures

	Baseline STAS	Stimulated STAS	Achieved Market Share
LF	2.5	3.0	2.7
JC	7.0	11.7	8.2*
LCC	3.0	4.7	2.8
DD	7.8	8.4	8.4
AK	2.6	4.7	3.6*
LC	7.1	7.1	4.3
LJ	2.1	2.1	1.6
AE	8.3	9.9	5.8
BD	6.2	9.5	6.7
CH	3.3	4.0	4.6*
DH	3.4	5.3	3.2
LD	4.7	5.2	3.6
MG	1.5	2.2	2.4*
AL	3.0	4.8	3.3*
BP	3.3	4.9	4.5*
KD	3.1	3.6	3.7*
EE	5.2	10.6	7.3*
KG	1.2	1.7	2.3*
LG	2.4	2.9	2.8*
LCCC	1.6	1.9	1.6
BR	2.4	3.2	2.5
KH	3.3	3.5	1.9
AJ	3.7	8.6	3.8
CD	7.2	13.9	8.9*
AH	4.9	12.4	5.7*
CN	3.9	5.9	3.3
All brands	4.0	6.0	4.2

*Brands with a minimum of 10-percent lift from Baseline STAS to achieved market share.

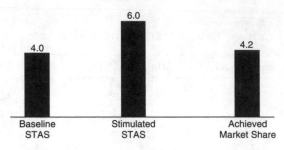

FIGURE 8–2
Trio of market share measures: Averages for Alpha One Brands.

Aggregate Effect of Short-Term and Long-Term Stimuli

Table 8–9 has five noteworthy features.

1. The brands all have a positive STAS Differential (this is of course a characteristic of all Alpha One brands).
2. In most cases the difference between the Baseline STAS and the achieved market share is relatively small. On average, the achieved market share is 5 percent higher.
3. The relatively small average difference between Baseline STAS and achieved market share is less important than the fact that the achieved market share always represents an improvement in the second, third, and fourth quarters over the first quarter level. This improvement demonstrates the effectiveness of the various marketing stimuli.
4. The fourth point relates to the most powerful brands in the short plus long term. All the brands in the Alpha One group are successful in the sense that their advertising campaigns are creatively effective. In addition, there is some upward progress in their market share over the course of the year. However, judged by the rigorous criterion of the extent by which the achieved market share exceeds the Baseline STAS, the average lift is, as already mentioned, only 5 percent. But some brands achieve a minimum lift of 10 percent. These are marked with an asterisk in Table 8–9.
5. Two-thirds of the brands in this very successful group achieve a lift of at least 20 percent between Baseline STAS and achieved market share. About half this increase is a result of synergy between the various marketing inputs.

Separating the Long-Term from the Short-Term Effects

Since the increase (if any) from a brand's Baseline STAS to its Stimulated STAS isolates the short-term creative effect of its advertising campaign, it follows logically that any change from the Stimulated STAS to the achieved market share captures the long-term effect of the campaign, against the efforts of competitive brands.

This competitive activity inhibits most brands, so that although the STAS Differential is positive (for the Alpha One group), there is a drop between the Stimulated STAS and the achieved market share. The standard pattern is the rise and fall illustrated in Figure 8–2.

In their drop from Stimulated STAS to achieved market share, some brands hold up better than others. The twelve more successful ones are analyzed in Table 8–10. (In this book these will be referred to as the top performance brands). The fourteen less successful appear in Table 8–11. These tables are a real measure of the

TABLE 8–10

Brands that Most Successfully Maintain Their Stimulated STAS: the Top Performance Brands

Brand	Percentage Change from Stimulated STAS to Market Share	Advertising Intensity (% Points)	Price (Index)
LF	−10	2.6	110
DD	=	2.2	157
AK	−23	1.2	66
LJ	−24	3.3	88
CH	+15	2.4	143
MG	+9	7.1	130
BP	−8	1.9	90
KD	+3	5.2	87
KG	+35	2.7	113
LG	−3	2.2	127
LCCC	−16	4.6	123
BR	−22	5.0	109
Average	−4	3.4	112

effectiveness of *those parts of the marketing mix other than the creative content of the campaign.*

Two important points emerge from Tables 8–10 and 8–11.

First, as might be expected, the top performance brands have on average relatively higher advertising investments. The difference between an average advertising intensity of 3.4 percent and one of 2.5 percent is large, and would in most cases represent considerable dollar amounts. This means that the schedules of the more successful brands have the funds to provide greater continuity, thus helping to maintain these brands' ups against the advertising and promotional activities of competitors.

The second feature relates to price. The average price of the top performance brands is 22 percent more than the less successful

TABLE 8–11
Brands that Are Less Successful in Maintaining Their Stimulated STAS

Brand	Percentage Change from Stimulated STAS to Market Share	Advertising Intensity (% Points)	Price (Index)
JC	–30	0.9	101
LCC	–40	2.6	130
LC	–39	2.0	91
AE	–41	2.0	157
BD	–30	0.5	95
DH	–40	2.8	75
LD	–31	3.3	88
AL	–31	3.4	73
EE	–31	1.0	94
KH	–46	0.4	75
AJ	–56	1.2	81
CD	–36	2.0	82
AH	–54	3.5	97
CN	–46	9.0	46
Average	–39	2.5	92

ones (20 percentaged on 92). This indicates that buyers value the successful brands more than do the buyers of the less successful brands. This agrees completely with the theory outlined in Chapter 6 describing how advertising generates a long-term effect. Successful advertising builds added values. It works in cooperation with repeat purchase. And the value of the brand is gradually but significantly augmented in the minds of its users. They will pay more money for it.

Twelve Things We Have Learned About the Alpha One Brands

1. In an initial topline analysis, the three main marketing stimuli—the creative content, the advertising budget and the promotions—affect the seventy-eight advertised brands in this research in a remarkably similar way.
2. The Alpha One group comprises twenty-six brands with a combination of positive STAS and market share growth. Within this group, there is much variability among the STAS Differentials and the share improvements, but in many cases both are pronounced.
3. More manufacturers follow a price/promotional strategy than follow an advertising-driven strategy, although there is some overlap between the two.
4. When we examine the aggregate effect of all marketing stimuli, the long-term outcome of the price/promotional strategy is not much different from that of the advertising-driven strategy. (Promotions are almost always more effective in the short term, when measured in sales. They are, however, generally unprofitable).
5. The brands that are driven by a double strategy of advertising plus promotions generate a powerful synergy.
6. The only marketing input that is reasonably correlated with (and therefore probably predictive of) market share growth is advertising intensity—advertising pressure and market share follow one another in a crude but quite unmistakable fashion. This confirms a number of other studies that demonstrate the same phenomenon.

7. When we compare the trio of market share measures, the normal pattern (for the Alpha One brands at least) is a rise from the Baseline STAS to the Stimulated STAS, followed by a fall to the achieved market share, which represents the brand's response to pressure from competitive brands.

8. After discounting the short-term rise and fall, the net rise from Baseline STAS to achieved market share is on average only 5 percent. But for twelve of the twenty-six brands, it is larger. This is a reflection of the above-average success of those brands' marketing mix in a competitive marketplace.

9. For the twelve more successful brands, two-thirds show a lift of at least 20 percent from Baseline STAS to achieved market share. I believe that a substantial amount of this increase is caused by synergy between the different marketing stimuli.

10. There is almost always a decline from the level of the Stimulated STAS to the achieved market share, caused by the activities of competitive brands. But some brands fall less than others, as a consequence of the greater *long-term productivity* of their marketing stimuli.

11. As can be seen in Tables 8–10 and 8–11, the top performance brands (i.e., those that show the smallest drop from Stimulated STAS to achieved market share) are significantly more advertising-driven than the less successful ones. There is an even more remarkable correlation. The top performance brands—those driven by advertising investment—are able to support a much higher price than the less successful brands.

12. In this analysis, therefore, when we look at the overall progress of all the brands, advertising plays a marginally more decisive role in achieving sales successes than do the other sales stimuli, although there is strong synergy between all the marketing inputs when they are applied together. However, when we isolate the specific long-term factors (as opposed to the short-term ones), and when we in turn isolate the top performance brands, these are advertising-driven to a decisive degree. And the resultant improvement in value perceptions on the part of consumers leads to these brands commanding significantly higher prices than the less successful brands can. The apparent inner strength and drive—the internal momentum—of these

brands means that they do not require heavy and unprofitable promotions to boost their sales. The brands in this very special top performance group total twelve out of our overall sample of seventy-eight.

The points listed above all hold important operational lessons for advertisers, detailed in Chapter 13.

9

Advertising that Stops Working:
The Alpha Two Brands

The defining feature of the Alpha Two brands is that they combine a positive STAS Differential (i.e., short-term share improvement) with no improvement in long-term market share. There is undeniable evidence that their advertising campaigns yield results within seven days. But something intervenes to prevent this positive effect from being carried forward over the course of a year. Hence the title of this chapter.

The best way to describe this dissonance between short-term effectiveness and long-term lack of effectiveness is to examine the averages of the Alpha Two brands' trio of market share measures, together with the average index of market share growth. These figures can then be compared with those for the Alpha One brands. (Table 9–1).

Table 9–1 shows that the STAS Differential index is weaker for the Alpha Two brands than for Alpha One. But the major difference between the two groups is the negative trend in market share for Alpha Two, compared with the strongly positive trend for Alpha One. Remember that the market share growth shows each brand's development over the course of the year and is independent of the STAS Differential, although the latter is one factor that influences it.

With the Alpha One brands, the STAS effect works in conjunction with the other marketing stimuli to push sales upward. But the Alpha Two brands, despite their positive STAS, are clearly inhibited by failures in some parts of their marketing inputs, which depress growth.

TABLE 9-1

Alpha One and Alpha Two—Trio of Market Share Measures

	Average Baseline STAS	Average Stimulated STAS	Average Achieved Market Share	Average Index of Long-Term Market Share Growth/Decline
Alpha One	4.0 (=100)	6.0 (=150)	4.2 (=105)	129
Alpha Two	4.5 (=100)	5.9 (=131)	4.1 (=91)	83

Table 9-2 summarizes the main details of the nineteen brands that make up the Alpha Two group. They are ranked according to the steepness of their share decline, starting with the most depressed brand.

If we compare the Alpha One brands (Table 8-4) with Alpha Two (Table 9-2) we see that:

- There are more Alpha One brands (twenty-six compared with nineteen).
- The average Alpha One brand grew by 29 percent; the average Alpha Two brand fell by 17 percent.
- The average STAS Differential of the Alpha One brands is greater than that of the Alpha Two brands.[1]
- The average promotional intensity of the two groups is almost identical.
- The average advertising intensity of the Alpha One brands is 32 percent ahead of Alpha Two (and only seven of the latter brands are above the Alpha Two average).
- The average price of the Alpha Two brands is 19 percent above their category average (the comparable figure for Alpha One is 1 percent below). Since there is no difference in the promotional ratios of the two groups of brands, the higher prices of Alpha Two are a reflection of higher average list prices.

We can hypothesize that the weak sales performance of the Alpha Two brands is a result of their relatively low advertising volume allied to their high list price (despite the prevalence of reductions below the rather high average). Taken together, these two fac-

TABLE 9–2
Alpha Two Brands

Brand	Mark. Share 1st Qtr. '91 (% Points)	Long-Term Share Decline (Index)	STAS Diff. (Index)	Advertising Intensity (% Points)	Price (Index)	Promotional Intensity (Index)
BHH	7.3	42	121	1.6	116	88
LK	2.1	67	225	2.4	118	85
LE	4.3	74	121	2.1	110	106
CF	7.1	75	102	1.5	130	98
DE	6.4	75	111	2.3	155	81
AF	5.7	75	120	0.7	170	99
MF	2.9	76	102	1.7	91	188
LL	1.7	82	245	2.9	128	113
DF	4.7	83	118	2.8	92	116
AD	9.3	88	111	0.5	92	128
CJ	3.8	89	108	2.1	105	123
CE	8.2	90	124	1.7	144	93
JG	3.2	91	300	1.9	124	115
CG	5.6	95	102	0.7	137	98
MK	2.0	95	105	6.5	100	160
MB	7.8	96	114	2.4	135	126
AM	2.8	96	141	4.3	114	157
JF	3.2	97	187	1.6	81	96
LB	5.4	98	142	1.5	122	82
Aver.	4.9	83	142	2.2	119	113

tors are strong enough to negate the positive STAS Differential of the Alpha Two brands.

So much for the bare bones. But in the same way as I treated the Alpha One brands, we can get additional insights by doing some averaging.

In the analyses of the Alpha One brands, I looked first at the different amounts of the various marketing stimuli, to try and find out whether above-average quantities of these inputs generated above-average share growth. This was done in Table 8–5, and it led in turn to a number of conclusions. Among these was the discovery of strong synergy between the different marketing inputs (Table 8–6).

Unfortunately, the data for the Alpha Two brands do not yield differences as important as those discovered for Alpha One. However, the third analysis I made of the Alpha One brands rang a bell when it was applied to Alpha Two.

The Stimuli that Best Explain Different Rates of Decline

In the third analysis of the Alpha One brands, I isolated each brand's share growth as the dependent variable, and clustered the Alpha One brands into subgroups based on this. I then worked out the average intensities or quantities of the different marketing inputs for the brands in each subgroup (Tables 8–7 and 8–8).

In a similar fashion, I have divided the Alpha Two brands, breaking them down into two subgroups representing the brands that declined most (bottom ten brands) and those that declined least (top nine brands). I then calculated the average intensity or quantity of each marketing stimulus for each group. (Table 9–3).

The variations in the advertising-related measures are particularly evident. This is especially true of the large difference in the advertising intensity—a difference of 0.6 percentage points on a base of 1.9 (a 32-percent lift). This would translate into millions of dollars spent when applied to individual brands. This is a geared effect that can be illustrated with the following hypothetical example.

TABLE 9–3
Alpha Two—Bottom Ten/Top Nine Brands

Sub-Group	Long-Term Share Decline (Index)	STAS Diff. (Index)	Advertising Intensity (% Points)	Price (Index)	Promotional Intensity (Index)
Bottom ten brands	74	138	1.9	120	110
Top nine brands	94	147	2.5	118	117

If a brand with a 2-percent share of market accounts for 3.8 percent share of voice in its category, an increase of 32 percent in advertising intensity (from the base of 3.8 percent) lifts its share of voice to 5.0 percent.

If the total advertising expenditure in the category is $200 million, the brand's expenditure now totals $10 million, or $2.4 million more than it was originally spending.

The brand's advertising intensity moves up from 1.9 percent to 2.5 percent.

Another feature of Table 9–3 is the insensitivity of price as an indication of long-term marketplace success.

There is more to be found in the data in Table 9–3, and we can get to this by amalgamating all the information from the Alpha One and Alpha Two brands (Tables 8–7 and 9–3 respectively). These groups of brands have an essential point in common that they contain only those brands with a positive STAS Differential: They all have campaigns that are demonstrably effective in the short term.

The two subgroups of Alpha Two brands form a continuum when added to the three subgroups of Alpha One. All the brands follow a progression from the least to the most successful when classified by share change: the least successful being the bottom of Alpha Two and the most successful being the top of Alpha One. Fortuitously, the five groups of brands, all of them of approximately similar size, make up a quintile analysis covering the range of forty-five Alpha brands. This is a single analysis into five groups of brands, based on their success in the marketplace measured by long-term share growth. For each quintile, I have given the average reading for STAS Differential, advertising intensity, price, and promotional intensity. These data appear in Table 9–4.

Table 9–5 indexes the figures in each column, the bottom quintile being given the value of 100.

The first thing to note is that the only marketing input that comes near to predicting the extent of the market share growth is advertising intensity. This point comes clearly from a chart of the data illustrating the maximum points in each of the five series of numbers (Figure 9–1). Quintile by quintile, advertising intensity and market share growth are much more directly in step than is the case with any of the other inputs. The influence of these stimuli on

TABLE 9–4
Alpha Brands—Quintile Analysis

Quintile	Long-Term Share Growth/ Decline (Index)	STAS Differential (Index)	Advertising Intensity (% Points)	Price (Index)	Promotional Intensity (Index)
1st (Bottom ten Alpha Two)	74	138	1.9	120	110
2nd (Top nine Alpha Two)	94	147	2.5	118	117
3rd (Bottom nine Alpha One)	105	134	1.9	105	117
4th (Middle eight Alpha One)	115	144	3.3	97	103
5th (Top nine Alpha One)	167	161	3.4	95	116

TABLE 9–5
Alpha Brands—Quintile Analysis, Indexed

Quintile	Long-Term Share Growth/ Decline	STAS Differential	Advertising Intensity	Price	Promotional Intensity
1st (Bottom ten Alpha Two)	100	100	100	100	100
2nd (Top nine Alpha Two)	127	106	132	98	106
3rd (Bottom nine Alpha One)	142	97	100	88	106
4th (Middle eight Alpha One)	155	104	174	81	94
5th (Top nine Alpha One)	226	117	179	79	105

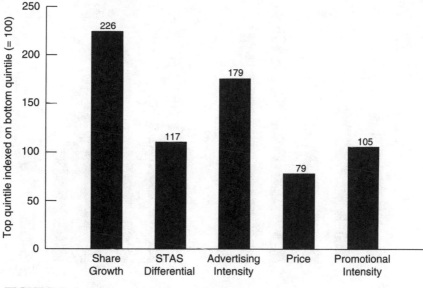

FIGURE 9–1
Alpha brands: Predictive power of four marketing stimuli.

sales is more *geared*, that is, in each case the change in sales is a multiple of the changes in STAS Differential, price, and promotional intensity.

The second thing to look at is the progression of the various marketing inputs, *in comparison with the change in market share.* In Figure 9–2, I have plotted advertising intensity and price against each quintile based on market share growth. I have ignored the other two inputs because including them would not have added much to the analysis: Readers can easily infer from the relatively small progression of the data for the STAS Differential and promotional intensity that they would produce flat curves. The progression of prices is less flat. And that for advertising intensity is very pronounced.

The advertising intensity figures contain one discontinuity, but their direction is clear enough. On the other hand, the rather flatter price trend is continuous. Readers will appreciate that the slope of the price trend is in the opposite direction to the advertising intensity trend, because the greatest sales are associated with the lowest price, but with the highest advertising intensity.

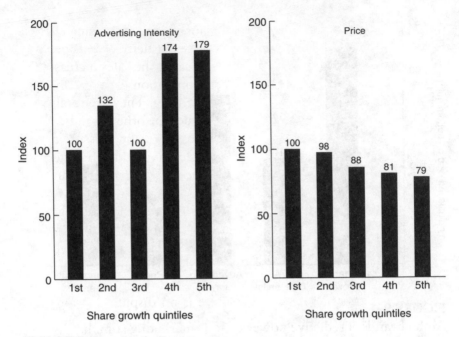

FIGURE 9–2
Alpha brands: Progression of advertising intensity and price effects.

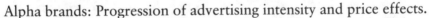

The really striking feature of Table 9–5 and Figure 9–2 is the steepness of the progressions. This represents the strength of the responsiveness of sales to changes in the marketing inputs: increases in advertising pressure and reductions in price. The slopes represent, in rather a crude form, the elasticity—or the degree of sensitivity—of the sales of the Alpha brands to changes in the two stimuli. From Table 9–5, we can calculate the following overall averages, which are of course based on the whole progressive run of forty-five Alpha brands:

Advertising. There is a 79-percent advertising increase (from 100 to 179), associated with a 126-percent share growth (from 100 to 226); these relative amounts of growth are in the ratio of 1.0 to 1.6.

Price. There is a 21-percent price decrease, associated with 126-percent share growth; these relative amounts represent a ratio of 1.0 to 6.0.

These ratios are the equivalent of a long-term advertising elasticity of +1.6 percent, and a long-term price elasticity of -6.0 percent. But the figures are not pure measures because the sales increases are the result of all the inputs working in cooperation with one another.

Nevertheless, these data are rather startling. They are totally out of line with what we know, from the study of other brands, about the responsiveness of sales to changes in advertising pressure and in price. Table 9–6 contains average figures computed from large samples of published cases, and the differences from the Alpha analysis are striking.[2]

What are the reasons for the massive difference in the degree of effect between the Alpha brands and the established averages? There are three interconnected explanations. The first two relate to the advertising elasticity; the third, to advertising and price.

First, there is the distinction between the short- and long-term effects of the marketing stimuli. There is no dispute that advertising's power to stimulate sales in the short term will generally lead to repeat purchase, which adds a lagged effect to the immediate sales trigger.[3] This explanation goes part of the way to explaining the difference between the two sets of figures, although long-term effects on their own could not be expected to add all the incremental sales we see in Table 9–6.

The second explanation derives from the fact that the published averages have been computed from a cross-section of brands in many studies, with no attempt to distinguish between the successful and the unsuccessful. In contrast, the Alpha brands are specially selected on the basis of the short-term effectiveness of their advertising campaigns. The average advertising elasticity for all brands, the low figure of +0.2, is a measure that has been pushed down by the

TABLE 9–6
Comparison of Advertising and Price Elasticities

	Published Averages—Short-Term Effect	Average of Alpha Brands—Long-Term Effect
Advertising	+0.2	+1.6
Price	−1.8	−6.0

nonperformance of the unproductive campaigns. The result for the effective campaigns is likely to be larger, perhaps much larger. However, until now, we have had no way of isolating the productive campaigns from the others.

The quintile analysis of the Alpha brands stretches out the range of effects, so that the sales performance of the most efficient campaigns becomes widely separated from that of the least efficient ones. The Alpha One brands have the intrinsic creative strength to boost sales in the short term. They contain a productive engine whose effect is boosted, perhaps multiplied, by media weight. To use the language of this book, media weight prolongs a brand's ups over the course of the year. This all causes the trend line to keep going up.

The first two reasons are reasonably persuasive. But the third reason is the decisively important one.

The published advertising and price elasticities are derived from regression analyses, which isolate the effect of advertising (and not price) and isolate the effect of price (and not advertising). The Alpha brands have not been treated in this way. On the contrary, the various marketing stimuli are seen to be working in conjunction with one another. As we saw in Table 8–6, there is in fact a powerful synergy at work.

The data from the Alpha brands point to the following chain of causality:

1. The STAS Differential is larger for the most successful brands.
2. Advertising intensity works on the STAS Differential, to generate a first degree of synergy.
3. The advertising effects (1 and 2) now work in cooperation with the price effect, to generate an even more powerful second stage of synergy, as illustrated in Figure 9–3.

Note that the initial impetus comes from the STAS Differential, which measures the short-term performance of the advertising. With an effective campaign, synergy is both possible and common although not universal. However, without an effective campaign synergy is impossible. Advertising intensity is wasted, and the powerful sales potential of price reductions is tamed and muted.

This analysis gives us a clear indication of why the Alpha Two

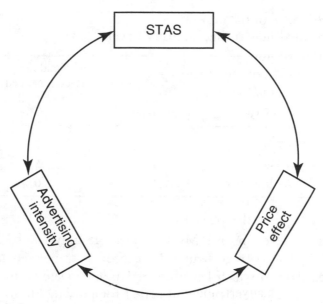

FIGURE 9–3
The triad of marketing stimuli.

brands have not performed in the long term. The factors that have rendered them ineffective are too little advertising pressure and too high prices. And the first of these explanations is the more important one.

Drawing an operational lesson from this conclusion is complicated by the fact that relative media expenditure is invariably governed by the size of the brand. Published aggregated studies demonstrate that the smaller the brand, the higher the share of voice, and the larger the brand, the lower the share of voice. And there is a fairly uniform gradation from small to large brands, with a continuous and progressive decline in share of voice.[4]

This analysis of average shares of voice covers successful and unsuccessful brands. Assessing the optimum advertising intensity for any brand is a judgment call, and each case is conditioned by special circumstances. But in general terms, if a brand is to grow, it is necessary not only for it to have a campaign that produces a positive STAS Differential, but also that it should spend at an above-average level. I believe that it should exceed the average for brands of a similar size by a minimum of 0.5 percentage points. For safety, I have

TABLE 9–7
Recommended Advertising Intensity Levels

Market Share	Average (% Points)	Minimal Levels Recommended for Growth (% Points)
1/2/3	3.5	4.0
4/5/6	1.8	3.5
7/8/9	1.3	2.0

rounded this level upward. My specific suggestions can be found in Table 9–7. The average figures have been extrapolated from the published data to which I have referred, and relate to the data in Figure 13–1. The levels recommended for growth (the right-hand column) are all well above the current levels for the Alpha Two brands (3.0, 1.7, and 1.5 percentage points respectively).

My hypothesis that the unsuccessful brands pull down the average advertising elasticity level to +0.2 has a parallel with the discussion in Chapter 4. I argued there that a single exposure of a successful campaign will have a positive effect. And I suggested that McDonald's data demonstrating the apparently negative effect of a single exposure were distorted by his being forced to aggregate the successful and unsuccessful campaigns into a single group.

Ten Factors that Account for the Different Sales Performance of the Alpha One and Alpha Two Brands

1. I believe the main factors that transform a short-term campaign effect into a long-term share improvement are those connected with a brand's advertising. First, there is its STAS Differential. Second, there is the brand's advertising intensity, which acts in synergy to prolong and augment advertising's short-term effect. (Tables 9–4 and 9–5).

2. Sensitivity to changes in advertising pressure is relevant to the long-term effects of advertising, not to the short-term ones.

3. Although the advertising inputs are the most important factors affecting share growth for the Alpha brands, there are demon-

strable advertising-related scale economies that apply to larger brands. Share of voice tends to be less for larger brands than for smaller ones. (Table 9–7). This causes some variation in the importance of advertising within the five quintiles of Alpha brands.

4. Strong synergy exists between the different marketing inputs. Their joint operation boosts the engine of campaign effectiveness. (Table 8–6).

5. The greatest influence of low price is its contribution to such synergy. This is something driven initially by advertising intensity, working in cooperation with the STAS Differential.

6. A lack of advertising intensity prevents the effective campaigns of the Alpha Two brands from driving market share upward in the long term. The lack of advertising intensity also inhibits the synergy between the different marketing stimuli for these brands.

7. The more a brand is able to maintain the momentum of its positive STAS Differential, the greater the relative importance of advertising. (Tables 8–10 and 8–11).

8. The more a brand is able to maintain the momentum of its positive STAS Differential, the smaller the relative importance of low prices. (Tables 8–10 and 8–11).

9. The differences in advertising intensity between the Alpha One and Alpha Two brands appear to be relatively small. However, the advertising intensity levels are geared, so that a difference of a fraction of a percentage point can translate into large dollar sums of advertising investment.

10. Based on paragraph 3, I have proposed the levels of advertising intensity necessary to cause sales of Alpha brands to increase, with different suggested levels for brands of different sizes. Each case needs to be judged on its merits, but my proposed rule of thumb is a minimal boost of 0.5 percentage points above the overall average for similar-sized brands. In many cases—for instance, for the Alpha Two brands—this would translate into a significant increase in share of voice and a considerable boost in advertising investment. (Table 9–7).

10

Advertising that Works in Some Cases: The Beta Brands

The Beta brands are the twenty largest of the seventy-eight advertising brands studied in this research. I have defined a large brand as one with a market share of 10 percent or more. In the whole field of packaged goods in the United States, such brands represent about one-third of all advertised brands, which means that the sample of large brands in this research is a little below the national average.[1]

Most of my professional life was devoted to large brands, and I gradually learned that they differ from the normal run of brands in more respects than in their size alone. In analyzing large brands, we need to bear in mind six special characteristics, and it is because of these that I decided to separate the large brands in this inquiry and treat them as a special group.

1. Sales of large brands tend to be more sluggish than the general average for all brands. Year by year, their sales do not generally change much; and there are more than a few cases of large brands that have kept their market shares intact for decades. The reason the shares of large brands tend to remain static, and in particular not to increase greatly, is their large volume. A 1- or 2-percent increase in the sales of a large brand generally means a large and sometimes massive incremental quantity of merchandise, and it is obviously much more difficult to sell this than it is to increase the sales of a small brand by 1 or 2 percent. Selling a given percentage extra gets progressively more difficult as a brand increases in size.

2. Because of the sometimes huge sales volumes of large brands it is often, if not always, a sign of success for them to hold their current position in the marketplace, particularly if the category is in decline, for example, cigarettes, coffee, dairy products, and hard liquor. If a brand holds sales in a falling category, its share of market of course goes up.

3. From one point of view, large brands are always under siege. They are invariably the targets of small brands, which are usually launched with the aim of taking business from subgroups of users of large brands, such as small numbers of consumers who may use and enjoy large brands but may be slightly discontented with the price, or the calorie content, or the range of flavors, and so forth. The marketing jargon for this type of competition is the launch of *flanker brands*. (These can either be new brands or variants of existing ones).

4. Manufacturers of large brands have too often responded to this type of competition by adopting the most dangerous course of action possible: a strategy that increases their vulnerability. Manufacturers have splintered their large brands into groups of subbrands to cover subcategories of users. In the United States, Coca-Cola now comes in eight separate varieties; Crest toothpaste in twenty-four; Tide laundry detergent in six. The alarming feature of this type of response is that it causes a breakup of the user base, and a loss of scale economies in production and marketing. One of the most counterproductive examples of the latter is the subdivision of advertising budgets into groups of sub-budgets, which are in total less effective than a unified budget for a brand.[2]

5. The scale economies of large brands are very real. In their application to marketing, such economies stem from certain important characteristics of consumer behavior; and they are expressed by the way in which large brands can use their advertising budgets more productively than small brands can.

Two behavioral characteristics distinguish large brands from small brands. The most important is their penetration, or their user-base—a large brand has more users than a small brand has. However, once a brand exceeds a certain size—normally about a 10-percent share—the brand's purchase frequency also tends to increase over its previous level. People begin to use the brand more often. Some analysts describe this characteristic rather imprecisely as an increase in loyalty to the brand. I prefer to use the less emotive phrase I coined to describe it—the Penetration Supercharge.[3]

Because consumers are inclined to use large brands rather more often than they use small brands, the advertising for large brands need to work progressively less hard as a brand gets bigger. The advertising for a large brand becomes more productive than the advertising for a small brand. Hence the phenomenon discussed already in this book that the share of voice of small brands tends to be higher than that of large brands, and that share of voice falls progressively as brands get larger.[4]

6. Despite these real advantages, many if not most manufacturers are unable to keep their hands off their large brands. There is an unerring tendency to milk large brands: to give them insufficient attention and resources. In my experience, this has been by far the leading cause of the eventual decline and occasional demise of many large brands. Milking is partly induced by a widespread and dangerous belief in the inevitability of the downward phase of a brand's life cycle. Many—although not all—manufacturers believe that their large brands will erode sooner or later, and they therefore undersupport them because they do not have faith in the brands' future. This policy will of course cause them to lose sales.[5] The reason for withdrawing support is however often more pragmatic. Manufacturers set great store by new brand launches, despite the failure of most new brands. All new brand ventures call for major upfront investments in research and development, in production, and in marketing, and these activities are most commonly funded by reductions of support behind existing large brands.[6]

A Bird's-Eye View of the Beta Brands

The details of the individual Beta brands can be seen in Table 10–1. Table 10–2 compares Beta with the average measures for Alpha One and Alpha Two. And Table 10–3 compares the trio of market share measures for all three groups of brands.

Comparing the Beta brands with Alpha One and Alpha Two, the former are not only larger, but they are also more stable. Moreover, there is evidence of smaller contributions from the various marketing inputs. Although the range of market shares of the Beta brands is very wide—from 10.4 percent to 38.1 percent—the range of the

TABLE 10–1
Beta Brands

Brand	Market Share 1st Qtr. 1991 (% Points)	Long-Term Share Growth/ Decline (Index)	STAS Differential (Index)	Advertising Intensity (% Points)	Price (Index)	Promotional Intensity (Index)
CC	10.4	85	89	0.5	114	100
BF	12.3	89	86	0.8	92	82
EB	19.0	89	93	2.5	110	120
CA	15.7	89	98	0.5	117	100
HB	23.6	92	116	1.4	104	131
HC	19.8	92	134	1.1	99	102
AAA	10.9	93	95	1.3	120	94
KAA	13.7	93	109	0.2	121	109
CB	13.3	94	110	0.8	93	77
JB	17.9	95	103	1.3	100	115
KA	22.9	98*	96	1.1	118	108
EA	20.9	99*	126	1.2	138	97
GB	38.1	101*	95	1.4	115	97
AA	16.3	101*	97	0.9	131	94
KB	16.9	102**	107	1.3	124	105
MA	16.5	110**	107	1.1	128	150
HA	25.4	110**	117	1.7	110	118
BA	13.8	111*	96	1.2	132	101
JA	28.1	114**	105	0.9	117	93
DA	16.6	116**	122	0.3	52	98
Aver.	18.6	99	105	1.1	112	105

*Advertising effect possible.
**Advertising effect probable.

other measures covered in Table 10–1 is remarkably compact. This point is demonstrated in Table 10–4, which examines the spread of the various variables. For instance, the share change for the least successful Beta brand is an index of 85, and for the most successful,

TABLE 10–2

Comparison of Averages—Alpha One/Alpha Two/Beta Brands

Group	Market Share 1st Qtr. 1991 (% Points)	Long-Term Share Growth/ Decline (Index)	STAS Differential (Index)	Advertising Intensity (% Points)	Price (Index)	Promotional Intensity (Index)
Alpha One	3.5	129	147	2.9	99	112
Alpha Two	4.9	83	142	2.2	119	113
Beta	18.6	99	105	1.1	112	105

116, representing a range or spread of 31 index points. Table 10–4 shows a small spread, demonstrating a rather limited degree of variation brand by brand in comparison with Alpha One and Alpha Two.

The Beta brands, despite the wide variation in their size, are both very large and relatively static. This is seen in the charts of share change for Alpha One, Alpha Two, and Beta. (Figure 10–1). Figure 10–2 shows the relatively small short-term advertising effect for the Beta brands. But this is followed by a long-term improvement to the level of the achieved market share: a quite different pattern from the Alpha One and Alpha Two brands.

The strongest impressions of the Beta brands that come from Figures 10–1 and 10–2 are stability, inner strength, and gradual momentum, evidenced by the relative unimportance of the market-

TABLE 10–3

Alpha One/Alpha Two/Beta—Trio of Market Share Measures

	Average Baseline STAS	Average Stimulated STAS	Average Achieved Market Share	Average Index of Long-Term Market Share Growth/Decline
Alpha One	4.0 (=100)	6.0 (=150)	4.2 (=105)	129
Alpha Two	4.5 (=100)	5.9 (=131)	4.1 (=91)	83
Beta	16.7 (=100)	17.6 (=105)	18.6 (=111)	99

TABLE 10–4
Range of Inputs and Responses for Alpha and Beta Brands

	Alpha One	Alpha Two	Beta
Share Change in index points	230	56	31
STAS Differential in index points	153	198	48
Advertising Intensity in % points	8.6	6.0	2.3
Price in index points	111	89	86
Promotional Intensity in index points	99	107	73

ing inputs and by the modest but continuously upward sales trend. These characteristics are essentially the result of the large mass (and long history of most) of the Beta brands. The small increase from Baseline STAS to Stimulated STAS shows that advertising plays only a small part in generating immediate sales. And the promotional intensity is also very low. The high average price of the Beta

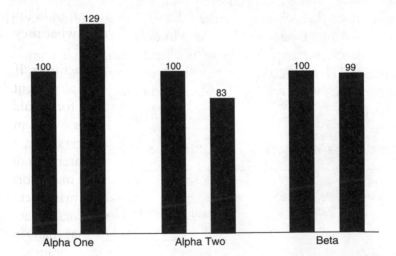

FIGURE 10–1
Alpha One/Alpha Two/Beta Brands: Share growth/decline (indexed).

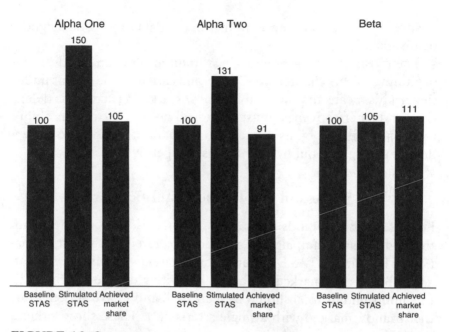

Alpha One Alpha Two Beta

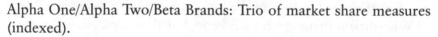

FIGURE 10–2
Alpha One/Alpha Two/Beta Brands: Trio of market share measures
(indexed).

brands is evidence both of their endemic strength and of high profitability. Users are prepared to pay higher prices for what they per-
ceive to be extra value.

High profitability represents a trade-off for manufacturers. If they
chose to stimulate sales more actively than they do at present, the
expense of the price incentives that would be called for would bite
into profitability to such a degree that the extra sales would probably not pay for themselves.[7] The wiser manufacturers (i.e., those
who do not milk their brands) are therefore content to invest
enough money in their Beta brands to enable them to make constant
sales and steady profits. Remember also the call on manufacturers'
resources made by new brand ventures, which are generally accord-
ed preference in investment decisions; this means that manufacturers' attention tends to be drawn away from their large brands.

Nevertheless, some Beta brands do better than others, and I shall
attempt to trace what has caused this. It is a difficult task, because
all the measures relating to the Beta brands tend to cluster around

the average. There are few extremes in the data to provide diagnostic insights.

The most important point to bear in mind is the one made at the beginning of this chapter: All Beta brands are to some extent under siege. This means that much if not most marketing activity is defensive, and its effectiveness must be judged not so much by its ability to boost share but by its capacity to maintain it, or even to slow a decline brought about by continuous competitive pressure.

The Successful and Unsuccessful Beta Brands

Five of the Beta brands are successful for reasons connected with their advertising campaigns: a fact demonstrated by their combination of a positive STAS Differential and market share improvement. These brands are marked in Table 10–1 with a double asterisk (**). I believe that this total should be increased, and I have added 5 further brands, marked with a single asterisk (*). These show either a constant or an upward share trend, despite a modestly negative STAS Differential in four of the five cases.

Why should these last brands be included as successes?

As I have already explained, it is difficult for the Beta brands to grow because of their large size. And when such brands do grow, this is the result of increased purchase frequency from existing users rather than from increased penetration: acquiring new users. The evidence from the research in this book is that advertising tends to have a slightly greater effect on regular users than on irregular ones. In my pilot work on the Nielsen data, I made the analysis shown in Table 10–5, which covers the ten advertised brands in the Packaged Detergents category.

In this particular analysis, I defined regular users of any particu-

TABLE 10–5
Analysis of Regular and Irregular Users—Ten Brands of Packaged Detergents

Average STAS Differential Index	151
STAS Differential Index—Regular Users	155
STAS Differential Index—Irregular Users	145

lar brand as users of only one or two brands in the category; irregular users are those who use three or more. I calculated the average STAS Differential for each brand for its regular and irregular users separately, and then averaged all the figures for the regular and the irregular groups.

The data show that advertising has a slightly greater effect on regular than on occasional users. We should not, however, conclude too much from Table 10–5, because the subsamples from which it was composed are small. But I believe that the direction of the figures is correct. And the regular/irregular distinction applies to the Beta brands covered by Table 10–5.

Since there is (at least) directional evidence that advertising that works in the short term operates more strongly on regular than occasional users, I believe on judgment that the advertising is working in this way with brands KA, EA, GB, AA, and BA, which have at least held their sales or modestly improved them, although their STAS Differential shows a small overall reduction in four of the five cases.

If readers accept my conclusion that advertising works effectively for ten of the Beta brands, then the total number of campaigns in this research which are successful in both the short and long term becomes thirty-six (twenty-six Alpha One plus ten Beta brands). These thirty-six represent (a projected) 46 percent of all advertised brands, or 25 percent of all brands advertised and unadvertised. As I said in Chapter 3, the guesses made almost a century ago by Lever and Wanamaker may have been slightly optimistic, but they were certainly not wide of the mark.

The Long-Term Role of Advertising

The most unusual feature of the Beta brands that has emerged from this analysis is their small but uninterrupted improvement in the trio of market share measures. (Table 10–3). The Beta brands do not move much, but the short-term campaign effect (+5 percent), is followed by a further progressive improvement over the course of the year (+6 percent). Note that these changes relate to growth of sales from the level of the Baseline STAS.[8]

The increase between Baseline STAS and achieved market share (a different measure from that used in Table 10–1), is a particularly sensitive indicator of advertising effect, and it suggests that this effect is in line with the theory propounded in Chapter 6: that advertising works progressively in cooperation with consumer satisfaction with the functional performance of the brand. This is a mutual reinforcement that boosts purchase frequency.

The way to test this hypothesis is to examine separately the two groups of Beta brands: those with successful advertising campaigns and those without them. As an aside, it is also interesting to contrast the successful Beta Brands (Table 10–6) with the successful Alpha One brands (Table 10–2). The reasons for the success of the Alpha One brands are very clear. It is a more complex procedure to ferret out why the more successful Beta brands have actually succeeded.

The most obvious feature of Table 10–6 is the considerable difference between the market share growth of the unsuccessful and successful Beta brands: The latter is 16 percent above the former. Is this caused purely by the greater internal momentum of the more successful brands?

Promotions do not appear to be important. And the overall influence of price (which embraces promotions) is nonexistent, since the average price of the more successful brands is 9 percent higher than the less successful ones. This is a further confirmation of the theory of advertising's long-term effect, just discussed.

We are left with the two advertising-related measures. But the STAS effect is small, and there is no apparent difference in advertising intensity. However, when we consider the latter, we must take into account the average size of the brands. The brands in the more successful subgroup are on average 38 percent larger than the unsuccessful ones. The share of voice of the larger brands should be

TABLE 10–6
Beta Brands—Unsuccessful/Successful Campaigns

Subgroup	Average Market Share (% Points)	Long-Term Share Growth/ Decline (Index)	STAS Differential (Index)	Advertising Intensity (% Points)	Price (Index)	Promotional Intensity (Index)
Ten unsuccessful	15.7	91	103	1.0	107	103
Ten successful	21.6	106	107	1.1	117	106

TABLE 10–7
Beta Brands—Advertising/Market Share Matrix

	Unsuccessful Brands	Successful Brands
Spend below-average for market share	6	2*
Spend above-average for market share	4	8

*This sub-group contains an exceptional brand, DA, which is driven by low price and is therefore (presumably) forced to cut back its advertising intensity.

on average below that of the smaller ones. Yet the observed advertising intensity is the same in the two groups. This point needs to be explored, although in doing so we shall be using some small sub-samples. In Table 10–7, the average levels of advertising support by which the Beta brands are compared are derived from Table 13–1.

The data in Table 10–7 are thin. They nonetheless provide some support for the hypothesis that advertising makes a difference to the successful Beta brands. The latter have a slightly higher STAS Differential, allied to a greater likelihood of higher advertising investment than the unsuccessful Beta brands.

Store Brands

Unadvertised store brands make an instructive comparison with the Beta brands. This research yielded data on nine store brands, although the actual brand names in each product category differed from store to store. This variability does not matter much in this analysis, since there are no advertising-created added values to consider, except for those that are the product of the store's name and reputation, which are the result of broader influences than advertising alone. I shall be concerned essentially with price, and the overall picture of the store brands is shown in Table 10–8.

The number of store brands in my sample (nine out of 142) is below the national average of 20 percent of all brands, representing 15 percent of aggregate dollar market share.[9] These figures indicate that store brands on average have a dollar share below volume

TABLE 10–8
Store Brands

Brand	Market Share 1st. Qtr. '91 (% Points)	Long-Term Share Growth (Index)	Price (Index)	Promotional Intensity (Index)
BQ	3.1	113	72	23
DQ	2.5	116	92	121
EQ	8.1	93	80	53
FQ	41.4	93	82	87
GQ	13.5	100	72	45
HQ	21.7	98	88	51
JQ	6.0	92	79	65
LQ	7.2	104	72	23
MQ	28.9	108	72	78
Average	14.7	102	79	61

share, which fits with their low prices. It also suggests that the concentration of this present research on larger brands goes some way to explaining the low representation of store brands.

In confirmation of this last point, the average market share of the nine store brands is rather lower than that for the Beta brands. The size distribution of the store brands is skewed, with five of them being much below the average. But even with this variability in size, the special situation of store brands, with their guarantee of distribution and display, gives them an internal impetus similar to that enjoyed by the Beta group.

The functional quality of store brands is generally satisfactory, although not exceptional. This, together with their distributional strength, provides momentum. The only marketing input that affects them demonstrably is their price. Since promotions play an extremely small role in marketing store brands, their low average cost to the consumer stems from their generally low list prices.

The average rate of growth of store brands is fractionally ahead of the Beta brands. But this progress is paid for by the profit foregone. The expense of manufacturing store brands is probably as a general rule a bit less than that of advertised brands as a consequence of their slightly lower product quality.[10] But their average price is 29 percent below Beta brands (79 compared with 112). It is unlikely that the total advertising investment plus trade promotional allowances of the Beta brands deflate revenue to such an extent. It is therefore reasonably certain that the Beta brands are more profitable to their manufacturers than many if not most store brands. As explained in Chapter 3, store brands are also likely to be less profitable to retailers than manufacturers' brands, although the markup may be higher.

Nine Factors that Explain the Performance of the Beta Brands

1. The Beta brands tend to be stable and profitable, as a result of both their large mass and the scale economies they generate.

2. The various marketing inputs play a smaller role with the Beta brands than with Alpha One and Alpha Two.

3. However, the Beta brands are always to some extent under siege, so that they require marketing support for defensive purposes.

4. The Beta brands show a modest increase from Baseline STAS to Stimulated STAS, and also to the third step, achieved market share. This progression suggests that the advertising for these brands reinforces the satisfaction felt by existing users and generates increased purchase frequency.

5. Five of the twenty Beta brands have demonstrably effective advertising campaigns. I believe that an additional five brands have campaigns that work in an essentially defensive fashion. Adding the ten effective Beta campaigns to the twenty-six effective Alpha One campaigns gives a total of thirty-six, or a (projected) success rate for advertising of forty-six percent of advertised brands.

6. The progress of the Beta brands is more a result of their internal momentum than is the case for Alpha One and Alpha Two. Advertising seems to work more as a reinforcement among the Beta group.

7. Promotions have little long-term influence on the Beta brands, and the most successful brands command on average a premium price, which is proof of the high esteem in which they are held by their users.

8.   Advertising plays some part in boosting the sales of the more successful Beta brands, but the supporting evidence for this is thin because of the small sizes of the subsamples.

9. Beta brands bear a resemblance to unadvertised store brands. But since the main engine driving store brands is their low list prices, store brands will in many if not most cases be less profitable than Beta brands, both to the manufacturer and the storekeeper.

11

Advertising that Does Not Work:
The Gamma Brands

The Gamma brands represent a relatively small group of thirteen names. Their most obvious characteristics can be seen in Table 11–1. They benefit from little share growth overall, although the patterns of increase and decline differ brand by brand.

The most important conclusions from Table 11–1 are those that relate to advertising. The STAS Differential shows a reduction from the Baseline, averaging 19 percent. This demonstrates that for these brands the short-term effect of advertising is negative: Their advertising is not strong enough to prevent a serious loss of business to competitive brands. Yet the advertising intensity of the Gamma brands is higher than that for any of the other groups. Since there is

TABLE 11–1

Comparison of Averages—Alpha One/Alpha Two/Beta/Gamma Brands

Group	Market Share 1st Quarter 1991 (% Points)	Long-Term Share Growth/ Decline (Index)	STAS Diff. (Index)	Advertising Intensity (% Points)	Price (Index)	Promotional Intensity (Index)
Alpha One	3.5	129	147	2.9	99	112
Alpha Two	4.9	83	142	2.2	119	113
Beta	18.6	99	105	1.1	112	105
Gamma	4.4	103	81	3.3	115	107

TABLE 11–2

Alpha One/Alpha Two/Beta/Gamma—Trio of Market Share Measures

	Average Baseline STAS	Average Stimulated STAS	Average Achieved Market Share	Average Index of Long-Term Share Growth/Decline
Alpha One	4.0 (=100)	6.0 (=150)	4.2 (=105)	129
Alpha Two	4.5 (=100)	5.9 (=131)	4.1 (=91)	83
Beta	16.7 (=100)	17.6 (=105)	18.6 (=111)	99
Gamma	5.5 (=100)	4.3 (=78)	4.5 (=82)	103

no overall share growth, the relatively high advertising intensity obviously does not compensate for the lack of advertising quality.

The weakness in the Stimulated STAS and the decline to achieved market share are more pronounced than for any of the other groups of brands (Table 11–2). Note that the Baseline STAS (5.5 percent) is significantly higher than the first quarter market share (4.4 percent in Table 11–1), suggesting that decline was under way from the very beginning of the year.

Measured by the change from first-quarter share to achieved market share, the brands hold their own in total. This overall stability was the end product of increases for some brands and declines for others. But since the advertising had no short-term effect, some other dynamics must be at work to boost the more successful brands. Yet the Gamma brands in general are neither underpriced nor overpromoted (Table 11–1). We must therefore look at the performance of individual brands for clues to why the more successful ones succeeded.

Table 11–3 describes the individual brands that make up the Gamma group. This table has a number of interesting features.

• The brands are almost evenly split between those that lost market share and those that gained. This range of the changes is reasonably large, from -23 percent to +35 percent.
• The STAS Differentials are all negative, with some skew in their distribution, four brands being below the Gamma mean and nine brands above it.

- As mentioned, the average advertising intensity is high: 3.3 percentage points, although the distribution is again skewed, with nine brands being below the Gamma mean and four brands above it. The overall range is exceptionally wide: from 0.1 to 14.2 percentage points.
- The average price of the Gamma brands is 15 percent above their category average, and eight of the brands are in turn higher than the Gamma average. The relatively high (effective) prices are a reflection of high list prices. This factor imposes a general brake on the Gamma brands.
- Average promotional intensity of the Gamma brands is 7 percent above their category average. Promotions do not have enough weight to compensate for the high list prices.

TABLE 11–3
Gamma Brands

Brand	Market Share 1st Qtr. 1991 (% Points)	Long-Term Share Growth/Dec. (Index)	STAS Differential (Index)	Advertising Intensity (% Points)	Price (Index)	Promotional Intensity (Index)
CO	3.0	77	94	1.0	117	136
BEE	3.5	80	67	3.1	120	120
KE	3.9	87	82	1.8	98	96
BN	6.4	89	93	3.9	119	113
DJ	2.8	97	84	1.1	68	133
KF	3.2	97	83	1.2	106	106
KBB	7.8	105	91	0.1	118	118
LA	5.3	109	85	1.9	64	108
EF	6.0	112	97	2.3	104	89
FA	7.7	114	44	3.5	128	125
MD	3.1	119	81	2.9	137	67
FE	2.6	123	76	14.2	147	105
DL	1.7	135	75	5.9	165	80
Average	4.4	103	81	3.3	115	107

• The Gamma brands are different from Alpha One and Alpha Two in that there is no decline from the level of the Stimulated STAS to achieved market share (Table 11–2). Since there is a pronounced dip from Baseline STAS to Stimulated STAS, there are no temporary sales increases to erode. And—unlike the Beta brands—there are no small temporary increments on which to build.

Why Are Some Gamma Brands Successful?

In the same way that I divided the Alpha One, Alpha Two, and Beta brands into subgroups, Table 11–4 divides the Gamma brands. The sample size of thirteen is unfortunately small, but there is a clear dividing line: between the subgroup of six brands that are declining, and the seven that are increasing.

Table 11–4 has one very puzzling feature. The theory of advertising described in Chapter 6, which was consistently supported by the data for the Alpha One, Alpha Two, and Beta brands, holds that the sales effect of advertising is triggered by the STAS Differential, and prolonged and augmented by advertising intensity. The theory also predicates that a negative STAS Differential, showing a clear absence of short-term sales effect, is incapable of boosting sales in the long term. However, the data from Table 11–4 that show that the more successful Gamma brands are more advertising intensive than the less successful ones, flies in the face of this theory. The

TABLE 11–4
Declining and Increasing Gamma Brands

Subgroup	Av. Market Share 1st Qtr. 1991 (% Points)	Av. Long-Term Share Growth/ Decline (Index)	Av. STAS Diff. (Index)	Av. Adertising Intensity (% Points)	Av. Price (Index)	Av. Promotional Intensity (Index)
Bottom six brands	3.8	88	84	2.0	105	117
Top seven brands	4.9	117	78	4.4	123	99

more successful Gamma brands appear to show that advertising is capable of a long-term effect without an initial short-term trigger.

However, there is one fact that denies this possibility. During 1992, only two of the seven growing Gamma brands continued to increase. If the growth of these brands during 1991 is a signal of long-term effect in the absence of short-term effect, why has this long-term stimulus not continued after the end of the year?

There must be other factors that have caused the growth during 1991. In fact, I believe that certain of the Gamma brands have special features, and that we can find other ways of explaining the sales increase of the top seven brands.

One brand (LA) is driven by an exceptionally low list price: the bottom (relative) price in the Gamma group. This is the obvious reason for LA's success in 1991; nevertheless the brand declined in 1992.

Two brands (KBB and DL) have highly visible brand names, because they are line extensions of other ubiquitous and successful products: either in the same category (KBB) or in a related category (DL). Sales success was due to a ruboff from the established and successful brands to the two Gamma brands. However, this factor was not strong enough to maintain the sales increase in 1992.

Three of the apparently successful Gamma brands are widely familiar because of their long history and prominence in the marketplace, which I believe to be greater than their sales levels suggest (EF, FA, and MD). In my opinion, the apparent buoyancy of these brands was partly the result of their "living off their fat." The identity of their manufacturers also suggests that these brands received substantial trade promotional support.

The advertising budgets of all three of these brands were deployed in an extremely unusual fashion: They were concentrated strongly into one quarter of the year. However, there is no evidence of extra sales in the periods of advertising concentration, suggesting that the brands were insensitive to changes in advertising pressure.

Interestingly enough, two of these three brands were soon in trouble. The sales of EF went down in 1992 and the brand was withdrawn from the market in 1993. FA (whose sales went up in 1992) was sold as a complete entity to another manufacturer.

One brand (FE) has a freak advertising intensity figure of 14.2 percentage points. This reading actually distorts the average advertising intensity for the top seven Gamma brands, and it certainly suggests that there is something wrong with the statistical sample for this brand. FE has a small sales volume, and I suspect that its apparent success is also distorted by sampling problems.

I believe overall that, although the Gamma brands do not provide positive support for the theory that a short-term effect is a necessary condition for advertising to be effective in the long term, they do not negate that theory. Most of the growing Gamma brands do not have any prolonged sales success, and the progress of a number of them in 1991 can be explained by reasons unconnected with the advertising.

Five Reasons Explaining the Performance of the Gamma Brands

1. The negative STAS Differential of all the Gamma brands exerts a downward pressure, and for six of the thirteen brands, there are no forces to counter it.

2. The Gamma brands are on average priced relatively high, and this acts as a brake on growth. However, individual brands are stimulated by low prices or high promotional intensity.

3. The marketplace performance of some Gamma brands raises the possibility that their sales success could be the product of high advertising intensity, despite the negative STAS. This suggests that advertising might work in the long term without any initial short-term impetus. But most of the growing Gamma brands did not continue to increase in 1992. And an examination of the individual brands suggests special reasons for the increases in 1991.

4. Since advertising has little influence on the Gamma brands, which are also priced rather high, there is no synergy between effective advertising and low prices.

5. The Gamma brands are stagnant overall. Half are declining, mainly because of deficient advertising quality. The increases in the remaining Gamma brands are driven by stimuli other than advertising.

12

Penetration and Purchase Frequency

This chapter has two objectives. It is written to remind advertising practitioners that:

1. Advertising is predominantly concerned with consumer behavior. And although advertising is capable of affecting such behavior significantly, it tends to be impeded in any attempt to *change* behavior by the innate uniformity and regularity of purchasing patterns. These are described in this chapter.
2. When a brand becomes established and joins the homemaker's repertoire, this uniformity/regularity of purchasing patterns contributes to maintaining the brand's position in the repertoire. The role of advertising therefore becomes increasingly protective and reinforcing. It aims to boost purchase frequency, not penetration.

The normal way of monitoring the effect of advertising is by measuring the sales of the advertised brand: through retail stores, or as brands enter the home. Yet there is no direct link between advertising and those sales, because advertising is addressed to consumers, and a number of factors can impede advertising's ability to induce consumers to act. It can be countered by the efforts of competitive brands; there may be large stocks of the brand in the home to absorb any increased demand; and the brand may not achieve full retail distribution so that the consumer's effort to buy it is frustrated. To get a more reliable picture of what advertising is accomplishing, we should therefore look not only at sales, but also at

TABLE 12–1
Sales and Consumer Behavior

Sales of a brand in a defined period =	Household population (A)
	× Penetration (B)
	× Purchase frequency (C)
	× Packs bought per purchase occasion (D)
	× Average size of pack (E)

measures of how advertising affects the underlying aspects of consumer behavior that govern sales.

The relationship between sales and the key measures of consumer behavior is expressed in a simple formula, which we see in Table 12–1. This formula, and the other analyses in this chapter, are based on the methods first developed by the British mathematician Andrew Ehrenberg, who has worked with large accumulations of data from the United States and a number of other countries.[1]

When we compare different brands in any product category using the formula in Table 12–1, we find no important differences as far as measures A, D, and E are concerned. The household population—whose buying would represent the strictly theoretical upper limit to any brand's sales—is the same for every national brand. People tend to purchase the same number of packs on every occasion, no matter what brand in the category they may be buying. And the packs of different brands are generally sold in more-or-less uniform sizes.[2]

We can therefore conclude that the sales of any brand are determined by the brand's penetration, which is a measure of the number of buyers who buy it at least once; and its purchase frequency, which measures how often they buy it in the period we are looking at. In this research, these two variables are measured in the following ways.

Penetration covers the full year 1991. When we measure penetration, there is an important technical reason for specifying the time period. A brand's penetration tends to be the same when measured in any individual periods of equal length, for example, January, February, or March. But as the time period itself is extended, penetration goes up: It is higher in all of 1991 than in January of 1991 alone. Penetration grows because some buyers buy the brand for the first time during each period. However, new buyers dwindle in numbers in succeeding periods, because increasing numbers of them have in fact bought the brand some time in the past; in other words they are really infrequent buyers rather than new buyers. This factor causes penetration to grow, but at a declining rate.

On the other hand, market share does not change greatly as the period is lengthened. When we extend the period, total category sales and sales of any particular brand increase approximately in step, so that the ratio between the two—which is the brand's market share—remains relatively constant. Market share in all of 1991 is approximately the same as in January 1991.

Purchase Frequency is based on volume sales per buyer. Since volume sales differ by category (not to speak of the differences between categories in the units used to measure sales), I have based the calculation on the category itself, by indexing each brand's volume sales per buyer on the average sales of all brands in its category. I call this calculation the purchase frequency index.[3]

Penetration and purchase frequency are significant measures, for two separate reasons. First, their relative importance varies according to the size of the brand, which means that their relevance to advertising strategy is determined to a large degree by market share. The most common example of this is that small brands are normally driven by a penetration-based strategy, while large brands are much more directed toward increasing purchase frequency.

The second reason for the importance of penetration and purchase frequency is that they are closely related to three further measures of consumer behavior: the frequency distribution of purchases and the patterns of repeat-purchase and multibrand buying. There are regular and uniform relationships, whose very consistency has enabled them to be modeled mathematically. This was part of Ehrenberg's groundbreaking work. His models were derived from a broad range of empirical data and were rooted in penetration and purchase frequency. However, the data in this chapter show that detectable changes have taken place since Ehrenberg made his original calculations. (Much of his information dates from before 1970).

TABLE 12–2
All Brands—Penetration and Purchase Frequency

Quintile	Average Market Share (% Points)	Average Penetration (% Points)	Purchase Frequency (Index)
1st	1.8	6.3	84
2nd	2.8	7.7	94
3rd	3.9	11.0	92
4th	6.8	18.6	97
5th	18.7	26.9	125

It is unnecessary to explain Ehrenberg's models in this chapter. However, I shall make a few comparisons between my findings and Ehrenberg's *observed* data (not the predictions of his models).

The 142 brands covered in this research are analyzed in Table 12–2. I have made a quintile analysis by ranking these brands by market share, based on their sales over the full year 1991.[4] This makes for a proper comparison with the penetration figures for the same period. The quintiles range from the smallest brands (first quintile) to the largest (fifth quintile).

The penetration growth is plotted in Figure 12–1. Here, penetration and market share are seen to progress upward together, showing that sales growth is essentially a function of growth in the numbers of buyers of a brand. However, Figure 12–1 also shows that the growth of penetration takes place at a declining rate as brands get bigger (for reasons already explained).

The decline in the rate of increase of penetration is demonstrated in Table 12–3, which calculates the ratios of market share/penetration. In this table, we can see a sharp decline for the biggest brands.

Since penetration growth becomes less important as a brand increases in share, the largest brands must obviously be driven by something else. This factor is increased purchase frequency. This is clear from Table 12–2, which shows that the major increase in purchase frequency takes place in the fifth quintile. And if we look exclusively at the figures for the twenty-five brands with a market share of 10 percent or more (the twenty Beta brands plus five unad-

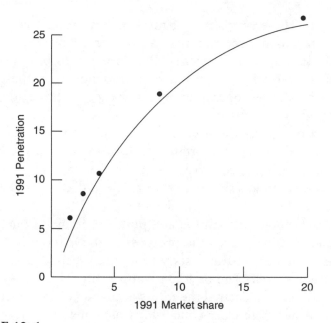

FIGURE 12–1
All brands: Penetration and market share.

vertised large brands), the purchase frequency index becomes even higher, at 127.

These data demonstrate an important aspect of the Penetration Supercharge, which was discussed in connection with the Beta brands in Chapter 10. As explained there, the growth of small brands is most strongly associated with increasing penetration; and purchase frequency does not change much as a brand grows to an

TABLE 12–3
All Brands—Market Share/Penetration Ratios

Quintile	Penetration (Market Share = 100)
1st	350
2nd	275
3rd	282
4th	273
5th	144

approximate 10-percent share of market. But when it gets to this level, its increased penetration is accompanied by a measurable step-up in its purchase frequency. People begin to buy the brand more often, primarily as a result of satisfaction with the brand's functional properties, operating in conjunction with the added values nurtured by advertising.

This process causes the pace of the brand's internal momentum to be increased, and an important result of this is that the brand's advertising does not need to work as hard to maintain or boost sales. Hence, a brand's share of voice tends to decline as its market share increases.

These facts about penetration and purchase frequency help us to understand the reasons for the progress in the marketplace of the seventy-eight advertised and sixty-four unadvertised brands covered in this research. The basic data appear in Table 12–4, and in Table 12–5 I have calculated the ratios of market share/penetration.

We can draw three clear conclusions plus one more speculative one from Tables 12–4 and 12–5.

1. The successful (but relatively small) Alpha One brands are driven by penetration, their ratio of market share/penetration being higher than for any other group. In comparison with Alpha One, the Alpha Two brands show a lower market share/penetration ratio—a reflection of their lack of staying power: their inability to maintain the impetus of their positive STAS Differential.

TABLE 12–4
Brand Groups—Penetration and Purchase Frequency

Group	No. of Brands	Average Market Share (% Points)	Average Penetration (% Points)	Purchase Frequency (Index)
Unadvertised	64	5.5	9.9	103
Alpha One	26	4.0	14.6	82
Alpha Two	19	4.4	12.0	89
Beta—successful	10	22.6	31.8	130
Beta—unsuccessful	10	14.7	26.1	121
Gamma	13	4.5	14.2	81

TABLE 12–5
Brand Groups—Market Share/Penetration Ratios

Group	Penetration (Market Share = 100)
Unadvertised	180
Alpha One	365
Alpha Two	272
Beat—growing	141
Beat—declining	178
Gamma	315

2. The Beta brands have a purchase frequency much above the average, and for the successful Beta brands it is higher still. This demonstrates that the driving force for these brands comes essentially from increased purchasing by existing buyers.

3. The unadvertised brands have a much lower penetration than for any of the groups of advertised brands. This is negative confirmation that advertising is a driving force for penetration (for all except the largest brands).

4. The fourth, and more speculative, conclusion from Tables 12–4 and 12–5 relates to the puzzling features of the unsuccessful group of Gamma brands. What has caused their relatively high market share/penetration ratio of 315? The Gamma brands, like the Alpha One brands, are relatively small, which suggests that the share/penetration ratio for the two groups might be broadly similar. But the argument in Chapter 11 raises an additional possibility. I believe that those Gamma brands that increased their sales were driven by forces other than their advertising, and these factors could explain the boost to penetration and purchase frequency seen in Table 12–4. On the other hand, the declining Gamma brands have figures below the Gamma average: a penetration of 10.2 percent and a purchase frequency index of 75. The poor sales performances of the declining Gamma brands are easy to understand from these relatively low numbers.

Frequency Distribution of Purchases

Analysts have known for decades that consumer purchasing in all categories of repeat-purchase packaged goods is skewed, with heavy buyers accounting for a disproportionately high percentage of sales volume. This concentration is normally expressed as the 80:20 Rule, which describes an approximation of the average distribution: the 80 percent of lightest buyers and the 20 percent of heaviest buyers of any brand each account for 50 percent of its sales.[5]

The data from the present investigation show that in the majority of cases, the degree of concentration of purchasing has increased since the 80:20 averages were originally estimated.[6] In Table 12–6, I have computed the share of purchases accounted for by the top 20 percent of buyers in each product category. In Table 12–7, I have analyzed the brands by groups.

TABLE 12–6
Product Categories—Frequency Distribution of Purchases of Average Brands

	Proportion of Purchases Accounted for by 20 Percent of Heaviest Buyers
Category	%
Packaged detergents	53
Liquid detergents	54
Bar soaps	50
Shampoos	53
Toilet tissue	46
Ice cream	58
Mayonnaise	52
Peanut butter	55
Ground coffee	55
Diet carbonated soft drinks	67
Breakfast cereals	52
Analgesics	59

TABLE 12–7
Brand Groups—Frequency Distribution of Purchases of Average Brands

	Proportion of Purchases Accounted for by 20 Percent of Heaviest Buyers
Group	%
Unadvertised	57
Alpha One	59
Alpha Two	57
Beta	60
Gamma	60

Most of the figures in Table 12–6 are marginally below those in Table 12–7, because they include the substantial numbers of All Others—brands that are individually not significant and not listed. Table 12–7 gives a truer picture of the frequency distribution of the more substantial and better established brands, whether or not they are advertised.

Table 12–7 shows clearly that the proportion of volume accounted for by heavy users has increased from the traditional 50 percent to almost 60 percent. And there is no reason to expect that the trend toward even greater concentration will reverse course in the future.

The advertising strategy for any brand normally embraces two objectives, although the relative weight given to each will differ brand by brand:

First, to increase penetration (especially important for small brands); and second, to increase purchase frequency by light users (particularly important for large brands).

The facts about frequency distribution suggest that all manufacturers should reconsider the balance between an offensive strategy (i.e., increasing business) and a defensive one (i.e., defending existing business). The facts about frequency distribution, and the probability that present trends will continue, apply to all brands, large and small. This strongly suggests that protection of the franchise should play a larger role in advertising than it appears to do in most cases today. Advertisers should remember that it is always a poor exchange to acquire as many as four new (light) users, if the price of this is the loss of only one existing (heavy) user.

The highest concentration ratios are probably mainly a result of past increases in purchase frequency for larger brands. This is certainly true of the Diet Carbonated Soft Drinks category; also of the Beta brands generally.

Repeat Buying

The rate of repeat buying for any brand is connected with the growth in its penetration.

When we compare periods that follow one another, the proportion of buyers of any brand in the first period who will buy it again in the next period, is remarkably uniform. The only qualification to this generalization is that the periods measured must be of equal length. The data in this chapter are quarterly figures, averaged across 1991.

The repeat purchase rates for the different product categories are in Table 12–8, and for the different brand groups, in Table 12–9.

Note three features of Tables 12–8 and 12–9.

1. Although there are variations in repeat purchase rates between product categories, the rates are 33 percent or more in every product category except shampoos, which operate in a crowded and hypercompetitive environment.

2. Surprisingly, the repeat buying rates are below the levels calculated by Ehrenberg, whose average quarterly repeat rates were mostly around 60 percent.[7] Ehrenberg's figures are illustrative and based on a small sample of brands; they may therefore not have been intended to describe general patterns. There is nevertheless quite a large difference between Ehrenberg and me. The only reason that occurs to me for the apparent lowering of the average repeat rates over the past two decades is that the more recent figures are connected with the increases in the concentration ratios. (Tables 12–6 and 12–7). Since light users, who represent 80 percent of purchasers, now account for a lower proportion of any brand's vol-

TABLE 12–8
Product Categories—Repeat Buying Rates of Average Brands

	Proportion of Purchasers in First Period who Repeat in Second Period
Category	%
Packaged detergents	38
Liquid detergents	36
Bar soaps	40
Shampoos	27
Toilet tissue	50
Ice cream	48
Mayonnaise	46
Peanut butter	41
Ground coffee	55
Diet carb. soft drinks	51
Breakfast cereals	47
Analgesics	33

TABLE 12–9
Brand Groups—Repeat Buying Rates of Average Brands

	Proportion of Purchasers in First Period who Repeat in Second Period
Group	%
Unadvertised	39
Alpha One	40
Alpha Two	37
Beta	49
Gamma	41

ume than in the past, it seems likely that their repeat purchase rates have fallen and brought down the averages.

3. The high figure for repeat purchase of the Beta brands fits with the high purchase frequency of these brands. Table 12–9 therefore demonstrates a second manifestation of the Penetration Supercharge. Not only do buyers of large brands buy them more often in a given period (Table 12–4), but the repeat buying rate from period to period is also higher (Table 12–9).

The actual relationship between repeat buying and penetration can be easily explained. Readers will remember that, in periods of the same length, a brand's penetration tends to remain constant. But as the measurement period is extended, penetration goes up. If in the first period the penetration of a brand is indexed at 100, a 40-percent repeat rate means that 40 percent of buyers carry over into the next period. The second period's penetration (the same level as in the first period), is therefore made up of 40 percent repeaters and 60 percent new buyers. The penetration in the first period was 100. The penetration in the first and second periods together is therefore now 160 (100 from the first period plus the 60 percent of new buyers in the second period).

As a specific example of this calculation, the quarterly penetration of Brand AA was 31 percent. With a repeat purchase rate of 41 percent, the brand's net penetration in two quarters was boosted to 49 percent (31 plus 18, which is 59 percent of 31).

Multibrand Buying

Multibrand buying applies generally to all product categories, and the number of buyers of two or more brands almost always exceeds the numbers of buyers of one brand (a group I shall refer to as sole buyers). The basic data collected in this research are set out in Table 12–10. The figures relate to the full year 1991. The phrase *brand repertoire* is used to describe the number of brands (sometimes also the names of the actual brands) bought by the consumer.

Table 12–11 gives fuller details of one typical product category: Packaged Detergents. This table breaks down the deal and nondeal purchases for buyers of different numbers of brands. As expected,

TABLE 12–10
Composition of the Brand Repertoire

	One Brand		Two Brands		Three or More Brands	
	Buyers % (Add Across)	Volume % (Add Across)	Buyers % (Add Across)	Volume % (Add Across)	Buyers % (Add Across)	Volume % (Add Across)
Packaged detergents	33	18	24	20	43	62
Liquid detergents	38	17	23	20	39	63
Bar soaps	30	17	25	20	45	63
Shampoos	33	12	24	17	43	71
Toilet tissue	18	11	16	12	66	77
Ice cream	31	15	28	22	41	63
Mayonnaise	55	39	31	36	14	25
Peanut butter	48	31	30	30	22	39
Ground coffee	32	15	22	19	46	66
Diet carbonated soft drinks	24	6	19	10	57	84
Breakfast cereals	6	1	7	2	87	97
Analgesics	43	23	29	29	28	48

buyers of many different brands tend to be more deal-driven than buyers of only a few. This applies with appropriate corrections to all categories. Ehrenberg has shown that existing buyers of a brand will take up most of the price promotions for it. Therefore people who buy many brands will be buyers of large amounts of promoted merchandise.

In Table 12–10, the proportions of buyers and the volume they bought are reasonably consistent across product categories, although four of the twelve categories show more extreme figures—toilet tissue and breakfast cereals with a wider brand repertoire, and mayonnaise and peanut butter, with a narrower one.

One aspect of the data demonstrates a change since Ehrenberg

TABLE 12–11
Brand Repertoire—Deal and Non Deal Purchases

	Packaged Detergents			
	Buyers % (Add Down)	Volume % (Add Down)	Deal Volume % (Add Across)	Non Deal Volume % (Add Across)
Total	100	100	38	62
Buyers of:				
One brand	33	18	28	72
Two brands	24	20	29	71
Three brands	14	16	37	63
Four brands	11	13	43	57
Five brands	6	10	39	61
Six brands or more	12	23	53	47

made his estimates of average patterns. As we saw with quarterly repeat purchase rates, Ehrenberg's figures are illustrative and based on a small sample of brands: therefore probably not intended to describe general averages. Nevertheless there are again quite large differences between Ehrenberg and me. My 1991 figures show that sole usage is now common: at levels ranging from 6 percent to 55 percent, with a median about 33 percent. Ehrenberg's average (for a forty-eight-week period) was 12 percent.[8] The reasons for the apparent increase in sole buying are not entirely clear, but there is presumably a connection with the increased concentration of purchasing among the heaviest 20 percent of buyers. (Tables 12–6 and 12–7).

Multibrand buying is a relatively consistent phenomenon, with one surprising aspect. There is a way of predicting what other brands are also bought by users of any particular brand in a category.

If we go through the laborious exercise of estimating how many buyers of one brand will also buy other identified brands, the patterns that emerge are illustrated in the matrix in Table 12–12. In this table I have stripped down the data to five brands in the bar soap category. I chose these brands and this category arbitrarily (my pilot work was confined to this product category).

The first horizontal line of figures shows the percentages of users of the first brands (also listed horizontally) who use CC: 23 percent of users of CD use CC; 22 percent of users of CE use CC; 21 percent of users of CF use CC, etc. There is approximate uniformity in the horizontal lines of figures, and these are averaged in the last vertical column (the averages include all the brands in the category, not just the five itemized in Table 12–12).

The averages in the last vertical column are related to the penetration of the brands to which they refer; in fact each is a multiple of its brand's penetration. CC has a penetration of 20 percent, so that its multiple is 1.2, a figure known as the *Duplication of Purchase Coefficient*.[9]

By multiplying a brand's penetration by its Duplication of Purchase Coefficient, we can estimate the proportion of buyers of any other brand in the category who will buy that brand.

The category averages of the Duplication of Purchase Coefficients are set out in Table 12–13. There are differences from category to category, but all the coefficients are of a similar order of magnitude.

TABLE 12–12

Duplication of Purchase: Proportion of Buyers of First Brand who also Buy Second Brand

First Brand / Second Brand	CC%	CD%	CE%	CF%	CG%	Average 14 Brands %
CC%	100	23	22	21	23	24
CD%	26	100	27	31	35	32
CE%	15	16	100	19	23	17
CF%	14	18	18	100	18	17
CG%	13	17	18	15	100	16

TABLE 12–13
Duplication of Purchase Coefficients

Packaged detergents	1.9
Liquid detergents	2.6
Bar soaps	1.4
Shampoos	1.7
Toilet tissue	1.2
Ice cream	1.2
Mayonnaise	1.6
Peanut butter	1.0
Ground coffee	2.0
Diet carbonated soft drinks	1.9
Breakfast cereals	1.4
Analgesics	1.2

The Long-Term Effect of a Brand's Internal Momentum

In my discussion of how advertising works in Chapter 6, I made the following points:-

In the short term, successful advertising is mainly driven by STAS, which is a measure of the creative effectiveness of the advertising campaign. The media selection and the budgetary weight do not play an important part at this stage. An initial STAS effect is a requirement for a long-term effect. A strong STAS Differential does not guarantee a long-term effect, but such an effect is impossible without one.

In the long term, STAS continues to play a role but it is joined by two additional factors. All three work in cooperation with one another, and sometimes manage to generate a strong and economic driving force that strengthens over time. The three factors are:

1. The continuation of the STAS effect.
2. Media continuity, which ensures that the brand has as many short-term ups as possible, to fight and neutralize the pressures of competitive brands. Media continuity depends on both the size of the advertising budget and on the method by which it is

deployed. This means that, within the individual flights, there must be enough concentration to ensure that most members of the target group are exposed to one advertisement for the brand. Given this proviso, the advertising must then be spread over as many weeks of the year as the budget will allow.

3. The brand's internal momentum. The strength and durability of this is governed by consumers' satisfaction with the brand's functional properties and whether they are in harmony with its nonfunctional added values, which are in turn both created and nurtured by advertising. Repeat purchase and added values resonate with one another to produce an incremental effect. This is measured by the proven ability of large brands to be supported with a share of voice that declines progressively as market share increases. It also explains why brands that are rich in added values are so often able to command a premium price.

This book has dealt fully with the first two of these factors. There is however information in the present chapter that can both illuminate and confirm the effectiveness of a brand's internal momentum.

Let me reiterate the point—which I believe to be essentially true—that this momentum is driven by the brand as a whole, and in particular by consumers' continuous experience of it, and not solely by the lagged effect of previous advertising. In my view, the latter is relevant only to the degree by which it has influenced the brand in the past. I am therefore extremely skeptical of the value of any measurement of the supposed long-term effect of advertising alone, especially when this is done by monitoring consumer perceptions, with all the intrinsic difficulties of that procedure: for example, some campaigns can be much more easily recalled than others because of their creative styles.[10]

The present chapter amplifies and supports the theory of internal momentum in at least ten ways:

1. Small brands are driven by penetration because the STAS effect attracts new users. Assuming that the brand is functionally distinctive and satisfies consumers, the brand now begins to develop an internal momentum, whose real payoff is in the long term.

2. The double evidence that most users buy more than one brand in any category and that duplication of purchase between all brands in a category is to be expected and can be calculated, underscores the importance of a brand's functional qualities. These have to be kept up-to-date and competitive. Consumers compare brands, and will discard unsatisfactory brands without any compunction at all.

3. The evidence that the largest brands benefit not only from higher penetration but also from greater purchase frequency than small brands, demonstrates the increasing momentum that can be generated by repeat purchase. This represents a scale economy of large brands. The fact I have just mentioned, that larger brands can be supported by a lower share of voice than small brands, demonstrates that advertising contributes to this scale effect. The combined operation of advertising and repeat purchase, and the demonstrably increasing productivity of this cooperation, is the first and most important manifestation of the Penetration Supercharge.

4. The skewed distribution of purchase frequency, and in particular the large and probably increasing share of purchases accounted for by the 20 percent of heaviest buyers, is evidence of the cumulative effect of the internal momentum of the more durable brands. These are not all necessarily large brands. Directing part of every brand's advertising to protecting the high purchase frequency of heavy users is an important means of maintaining a brand's internal momentum.

5. The higher level of repeat buying of the Beta brands is an additional manifestation of the Penetration Supercharge.

6. The growth during the past two decades in the proportion of sole buyers provides supporting evidence for the internal momentum of those brands that consumers use exclusively.

7. The most striking characteristic of the analyses of the frequency distribution of purchases and of repeat and multibrand buying is regularity. There is no way in which the patterns in Tables 12–6, through 12–13 could be haphazard. But it is a difficult matter to explain the reason for such regularity. The only sensible conclusion we can draw—and it is admittedly unoriginal—is that consumer preferences in the population comprise a complex web which is the unconscious product of the activities of manufacturers in the past, who were responsible for the construction of today's

product categories. Choice of brands is governed by these preferences, which cannot even be articulated by the consumers who determine them. The resulting patterns are pronounced, consistent
with one another, and slow to change. The best rationalization for
these uniform patterns is that buying is governed to a profound degree by habit. This is important to manufacturers for two reasons.

8. The first reason is that it is very hard to break consumers'
habits; and this explains the widely appreciated difficulty of
launching successful new brands.[11] The major problem is not so
much the initial launch, which may make short-term, temporary
progress. A strong manufacturer can force—or buy—retail distribution. Consumer sampling can be carried out fairly easily through
promotions. And advertising campaigns with a positive STAS Differential are not uncommon. The real difficulty of launching successful new brands lies in building the right combination of functional rewards and added values—a salient combination for
consumers which will start to build an internal momentum. The in-
tractability of this task is the probable reason why at least 90 percent of new brands fail.

9. The second reason the strength of consumer habits is very important to manufacturers is that habit represents a positive quality
that becomes very valuable to successful and established brands. A
brand's internal momentum, as it generates drive, eventually
achieves what seems to be the opposite effect: It builds consumer
inertia. The brand will now be bought as part of an unthinking
process, and will stubbornly remain in the homemaker's repertoire,
resisting the assaults of aggressive new brands. Brands have been
known to maintain modest places in the homemaker's repertoire
for years, sometimes even for decades, after advertising support has
been withdrawn. Manufacturers are, however, generally unconscious of the cost of such an operation: the profit they forego by
the price incentives necessary to keep unadvertised brands in distribution in the retail trade. (See the data on unadvertised brands in
Chapter 3, and on store brands in Chapter 10).

10. The last point in this chapter is the most important one.
Manufacturers who are educated into the unyielding and uniform
patterns of consumer purchasing may be led to believe that change
is impossible. They risk adopting a frame of mind that can best be

described as catatonic. They will become mute and passive, and unwilling to take action, effective or ineffective. The reality of markets is that, despite their apparent stability, they are actually kept in balance by the opposing aggressive actions of competitors: actions that end up by being substantially self-canceling. For a manufacturer to protect his position, he has to act with determination, although his only reward may be the maintenance of the status quo. But for any manufacturer to grow, what are needed today—as in the past—are superior resources, persistence, aggressiveness, imagination, and brains.

13

From Insight to Action

The key conclusions that emerge from this book are as follows:

1. The STAS Differential varies widely by brand. The strongest campaign can generate six times the amount of immediate sales as the weakest campaign.

2. Seventy percent (projected) of campaigns have a positive immediate effect on sales, but in many cases this effect is small in the short term and nonexistent in the long term. Sales of all brands are extremely volatile in the short term, so that the effect of a positive STAS Differential is often lost in the weeks when the brand is not advertised, because of pressures from competitive brands. As a result, the long-term success rate of advertising is reduced to 46 percent (projected) of cases.

The STAS Differential is a gatekeeper. Only if a brand has a positive STAS Differential will it have the opportunity to receive a number of further beneficial effects for the long term. The most important of these is that a brand might become an established member of the homemaker's repertoire, with inbuilt repeat purchase; the level of repeat purchasing increases when the brand achieves a 10-percent market share.

3. A positive STAS Differential enables the sales of a brand to respond to a single advertising exposure in the purchase interval. This makes possible the release of funds that can be used to advertise the brand more continuously, to the long-term advantage of the brand.

4. The synergy generated by a positive STAS Differential, working in cooperation with advertising intensity and low (promotional)

pricing, boosts the sales-generating effect of advertising intensity (if it were working alone) by a factor of eight.

This synergy triples the effectiveness of low, promotional prices (if they were working alone).

5. Effective advertising influences—but not exclusively—a brand's internal momentum. Effective advertising works in cooperation with a brand's functional distinctiveness compared to its competitors, to encourage repeat purchase.

One of the major benefits of a brand's internal momentum is that consumers will accept a higher price—which means that the brand can rely less on consumer promotions, to the benefit of the brand's profitability.

The best-performing campaigns support even higher consumer prices. Price can increase with growing degrees of advertising intensity.

A positive STAS Differential is a necessary but not exclusive condition for an advertising campaign to be successful in the long term. Advertising intensity—media continuity—goes a long way to transforming a short-term effect into a long-term one.

These points prompt certain types of action. In this chapter, I make specific recommendations, starting with the short term and ending with the extreme long term. I am addressing packaged goods companies and advertising agencies.

The Short-Term Effect of Advertising

1. The STAS Differential should be a gatekeeper for your campaigns. If a brand achieves a positive STAS Differential, you can safely make plans for prolonging the campaign's effect and turning a short-term into a long-term success. But if the brand does not achieve a positive STAS Differential, then you must immediately return to the drawing board.

2. The STAS data in this book are based on figures for the full year 1991. With large brands whose STAS is derived from large statistical subsamples, a STAS Differential could probably be calculated from six months' data. I recommend that in the future, pure single-source systems should be set up in test markets. Remember that many successful campaigns run for a number of years, and it is

worth spending time and money in the first year to ensure that the campaign is generating a measurable sales effect that will perhaps pay off over many years.

3. The STAS Differential should be used as a diagnostic device for a brand that is experiencing a sales softening. Assuming that the problem does not stem from causes unconnected with the brand's advertising (e.g., the successful relaunch of a competitive brand), the STAS Differential will tell whether there is an advertising problem caused by the creative content, or by the budgetary/media aspects of the campaign.

Creative Characteristics

4. The creative characteristics of successful campaigns are broadly definable. Use these characteristics to evaluate campaign ideas. They provide guideposts to judgment and a framework for communications research. These points are valuable tools for brand managers and other people responsible for advertising evaluation. They are less valuable as instructions for creative people, because this would almost certainly lead to stereotyped creative solutions.

Advertising Budgets

5. In setting an advertising budget, advertisers should be conscious of the average share of voice for brands of different sizes in any category. Average advertising intensity is only one measure that should be used to fix an advertising budget, but it is one of the more important ones. Share of voice falls progressively as a brand increases in market share. With the use of a simple statistical table, it is easy to establish a basic advertising intensity, which can be fine tuned by considering other marketplace factors relating to the brand. See Table 13–1. This table, which is intended to be user-friendly, proposes specific budgetary levels for brands of different sizes. These budgetary levels are expressed as share of voice.

6. Remember that the average shares of voice are calculated for a broad range of brands, most of which have stable market shares. For a brand to increase its market share, its advertising intensity should be higher than the levels set in Table 13–1.

TABLE 13–1

Average Advertising Intensity Ready-Reckoner

Share of Market	Share of Voice Above (+) or Below (–) Share of Market (% points)	Advertising Intensity (Share of Voice per Percentage Point of Market Share) (% points)
1	+5	6.0
2	+5	3.5
3	+5	2.7
4	+4	2.0
5	+4	1.8
6	+4	1.7
7	+2	1.3
8	+2	1.2
9	+2	1.2
10	+4	1.4
11	+4	1.4
12	+4	1.3
13	+1	1.1
14	+1	1.1
15	+1	1.1
16	+2	1.1
17	+2	1.1
18	+2	1.1
19	=	1.0
20	=	1.0
21	=	1.0
22	–3	0.9
23	–3	0.9
24	–3	0.9
25	–5	0.8
26	–5	0.8
27	–5	0.8
28	–5	0.8
29	–5	0.8
30	–5	0.8

Source: John Philip Jones, "Ad Spending: Maintaining Market Share," Harvard Business Review, January–February 1990, 38–42.

Media Continuity

7. It is important to determine what expenditure is necessary to ensure that most members of the target group are exposed to one advertisement in each period of advertising. Conventional notions of Effective Frequency—which support an average frequency level twice or three times what is suggested here—produce considerable waste because of the onset of diminishing returns.

8. The advertising flights should be deployed with maximum continuity: In many cases, advertising should be planned on a weekly basis. If gaps are necessary, make them coincide with seasonal lows in total category sales.

Advertising and Promotions

9. Do not advertise without some promotional support.

10. Do not promote without some advertising support.

11. The strategic planning of advertising and promotions should be integrated. Both activities should be timed to work in cooperation with one another, to maximize synergy. Creatively, advertising and promotions should communicate the same values as far as possible. This means that promotions should be used not only to generate sales but also for franchise building. Promotions therefore need to be conceived with more regard to building added values than is common in the field of consumer goods today. In other words, promotional ideas call for a creative input.

12. For the most successful campaigns, tip the balance gradually toward more advertising and fewer promotions. This should represent a long-term program to improve profitability and boost a brand's internal momentum.

Heavy Buyers

13. With every brand, part of the advertising and promotional effort should be directed at preserving the purchase frequency of the 20 percent of heaviest buyers. These people are likely to account for 60 percent of sales volume. This has creative, media, promotional, and packaging implications.

Internal Momentum

14. A brand's internal momentum represents its most permanent quality. A brand's longevity is a function of its internal momentum, and this momentum needs great effort to preserve and increase it. This means care, attention, and the investment of time and money. The downward phase of the brand life cycle is almost always caused by a lack of these inputs, stemming either from deliberate neglect or lack of attention.

15. Important brands should never be put on the back burner. Success for a large brand is often measured by the maintenance (not increase) of its market share, and this also calls for care, attention, and investment. The profits that result from the scale economies of large brands are substantial enough to justify such continuous effort.

16. A brand should be improved to maintain its functional distinctiveness, and such improvement should be part of a continuous program, including product testing the brand against its competitors. This is one of the most important ways in which existing brands (especially large ones) should be kept on a manufacturer's front burner.

17. Advertising campaigns should be refreshed regularly but should be consistent in the ways in which they project and nurture the brand's added values.

18. Every effort should be made to define the brand's added values. There are a number of projective research techniques that help us to understand added values in multidimensional terms.

New Brands

19. Pure single-source research can be used as a diagnostic tool for new brand launches. The STAS analysis will reveal whether or not the advertising campaign is effective. An estimate of advertising intensity will disclose any problems with advertising continuity. An analysis of repeat-purchase rates will point to difficulties unrelated to advertising such as functional inadequacies of the brand compared to its competitors, problems of price, or imperfections in retail distribution.

Research

20. A brand's development should be monitored by the progress of its penetration and purchase frequency. Evaluate occasionally the frequency distribution of its purchases, its repeat buying rate, and its duplication with other brands. Changes in the patterns of duplication can point to dangerous and perhaps unexpected inroads by competitive brands.

21. Consumers' perceptions of the brand's image attributes should be measured continuously to ensure that the brand's added values are being preserved and augmented, not eroded. This tracking is a vital diagnostic tool.

22. As much effort should be devoted to evaluating competitive brands as to evaluating your own brands. This should encompass both the functional properties and the added values.

23. The STAS Differential should be measured at intervals to check that the campaign still retains its competitive effectiveness.

24. An effort should be made to compute the price elasticity of every brand. This will help estimate the payoff of promotions in sales and profit. It will also guide you toward the optimum list price to maximize profitability.

25. One of the problems with research practice is its roots in the status quo. It is dedicated to improvements and refinements within the limits set by the current situation, and does not encourage big leaps into an unknown future. Manufacturers should encourage radically new types of research, despite the major costs—and the uncertain rewards—of such an endeavor. I am thinking about the exploration of what are, for marketing, untraditional fields. Such fields might be anthropology and symbiotics, which should be studied with the aim of generating hypotheses about the ways in which categories and brands might evolve, decades into the future. Such developments will inevitably be the responses to broad but gradual changes within society, and the marketing profession should be searching to identify these changes. This is the most subtle and competitive way in which the internal momentum of brands can be gradually boosted.

Appendices

Appendix A

Stability . . . and Volatility

In academic circles, marketing is sometimes spoken of as a scientific discipline. If it possesses such an unexpected intellectual respectability, a simple discovery dating from the early 1930s was what made it possible.

A scientific discipline is an activity with three special characteristics. It is based on an expanding body of accurate knowledge; it formulates and develops a doctrine derived from that knowledge; and the acolytes of the discipline have a mental attitude of objectivity and disinterestedness. Marketing was certainly not scientific until the discovery and widespread use of the Nielsen retail audit system, described in Appendix C.

A decade before World War II, this simple although expensive device transformed marketing guesswork into informed judgment based on a body of data. Nielsen made it possible to evaluate with reasonable precision the competitive relationships between brands, the ebb and flow of seasonal sales movements, and a host of detailed sales patterns and distributional variations according to type of store and region of the country. Nielsen did this by providing reliable standardized data by category and by brand and variety, from two-month period to two-month period, year in and year out.

Above all, Nielsen was able to trace the long-term sales trends in product categories, market segments, and individual brands. The Nielsen retail audit led to much enlightenment; and its influence, although not a hundred percent beneficial, was far more positive than negative.[1]

Smooth Sales Trends

Although Nielsen could measure many things, it was unable to detect short-term sales movements, for the obvious reason that the

163

measurement cycle was relatively infrequent: Stores were audited every two months. Nielsen was also inefficient at detecting advertising effects, except the very long-range ones. It did however generate crude but useful information on the results of promotions.

Nielsen data were presented in the form of simple charts covering extended periods, and the overwhelming impression made by these was that sales movements are smooth and regular. The information had an apparently seamless quality, which carried a strong implication for the consumer behavior underlying the sales changes that were being monitored.

Figure A–1 plots the sales of the two leading brands in a major category of repeat-purchase packaged goods over five years, 1975 through 1979. In the first year, the two brands are approximately equal in size; but by the fifth year, XB had slipped about 15 percent behind XA. Over the period, XA dipped slightly and then recovered; XB showed gradual erosion in the fourth and fifth years. Sales changed direction only once for each brand, and then only slightly.

The inevitable impression made by this analysis—which is typi-

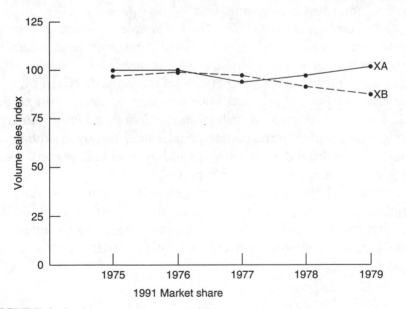

FIGURE A–1
Annual sales of brands XA and XB. (Index: Sales of XA in 1975 = 100).

cal of the type of annual data produced by the Nielsen retail audit system—is that over the whole five-year period, the same large number of purchasers had continued buying brand XA with approximately the same purchase frequency. XB had also remained a substantial brand, although there had been some reduction in the number of its buyers and/or in the frequency of their buying it, beginning about halfway through the period. This gradual weakening was connected with a fall in the advertising investment in XB.[2] Although the line of reasoning here is logical, I want to make a different point: When we compare individual observations that follow each other, all the movements are relatively small.

Figure A–1 is a microcosm of the stability of the entire process of marketing consumer goods. Many of the leading American brands of the 1920s kept the same dominant position for decades, and in many cases still retain this leadership today.[3] The large numbers of Nielsen retail audit analyses reported over the years served to reinforce the conclusion that market shares do not change much over time, and that any changes that do take place are slow, although often progressive (which gives them a long-term impact). The overwhelming impression created by the Nielsen data was an absence of radical change.

Since the Nielsen research system did not examine consumer behavior directly, only by inference, it was unable to examine some more subtle possibilities. When measured in consumer terms, a brand's sales in any period can be determined by a formula containing five elements, shown in Table A–1.

Of these five elements, the two most important ones—those that distinguish one brand from another—are penetration (the number

TABLE A–1
Sales and Consumer Behavior

Sales =	population
	× penetration
	× purchase frequency
	× packs bought per purchase occasion
	× average size of pack[4]

of households that buy the brand at least once) and purchase frequency (the average number of times they buy it). In different periods of equal length the penetration and purchase frequency figures for any brand remain relatively constant. But as we examine shorter intervals, the amount of variation is seen to increase. For instance, a homemaker's buying may be concentrated into one small part of a year: In the first quarter there may be heavy purchases driven by promotions, and nothing in the second, third, and fourth. When the annual figures are averaged, the result will be the same purchase frequency as in an earlier—or a later—year, during which her purchases might have been more evenly distributed over the four quarters.

Since most consumers have a repertoire of brands in each product category, a consumer may routinely change her patronage monthly, or even weekly. In other words, her purchases dart about between brands, either erratically or (more probably) in response to specific marketing stimuli.

The longer the period over which we review a brand's sales, the more these variations will even out. The constancy of purchasing patterns does not end with penetration and purchase frequency. Year after year (when we compare annual figures), there are similarly unchanging patterns in the frequency distribution of consumer purchases, in consumers' repeat-buying patterns, and in their multibrand buying: the interconnected web of brands that comprise each homemaker's purchasing repertoire.[5] These long-term constants were examined in Chapter 12.

There is, however, a general principle covering all continuous tracking in the marketplace. The longer the period covered by each observation, the smaller and smoother the transitions from number to number; and the shorter the period covered, the more erratic the movements from number to number.

One way of demonstrating this point is to look at Nielsen's bimonthly measures, which were the standard source of tactical market intelligence for more than half a century.

Figures A–2 and A–3 examine approximately the last two years covered by Figure A–1: the period during which Brand XB began to decline. Figure A–2 shows bimonthly data for Brand XA; Figure A–3, for Brand XB. The obvious feature of these two diagrams is

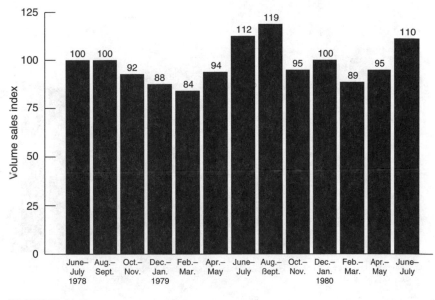

FIGURE A–2
Bimonthly sales of brand XA. (Index: Sales in First Period = 100).

that these readings are more variable than the annual ones. But the variations follow a regular pattern, driven by seasonal trends. Both brands peak in the summer, and the dip from summer peak to winter trough is approximately 30 percent, about the same for both brands. It is also possible to see how XA is maintaining its overall sales level, while XB is trending downward slightly. Note that the figures reverse course only in response to seasonal movements. There is no erratic flickering back and forth. The seasonal sales movements are entirely predictable from the experience of previous years.

From this sort of analysis, it is rarely possible to demonstrate any short-term effect of advertising. With Brands XA and XB, there is no correlation between bimonthly advertising expenditure figures and bimonthly sales. But promotions are another story. We can draw some clear inferences, although the measurement tool is a clumsy one. To look at the effect of promotions, we must analyze Brand XA's share of market. Figure A–4 ignores the absolute changes in the size of the category, period by period; each column

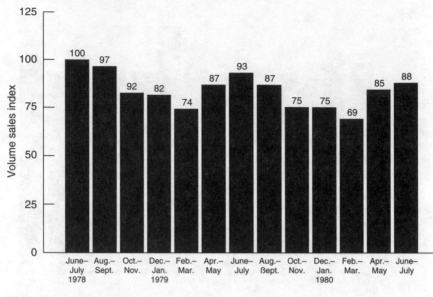

FIGURE A–3
Bimonthly sales of brand XB. (Index: sales in first period = 100).

would total 100 percent if all brands were measured. By plotting shares exclusively, as in Figure A–4, we can exclude seasonal effects, which muddy the water because promotions take place in both high and low seasons.

Two conclusions stand out from Figure A–4. First, Brand XA's market share is moving upward to a modest degree. We saw in Figure A–1 that when measured in absolute terms XA's sales were only going up fractionally between 1977 and 1979. Its increased share in this period must therefore be a result of something else as well: a very slight decline in the size of the category. This in fact is what happened in four of the two-monthly auditing periods covered in Figure A–4.

The second feature of Figure A–4 is a number of slight short-term ups and downs. The ups are associated with promotions: a loading of deal merchandise in the four months June through September 1979; and the combined effect of a number of specific deal activities, in particular special prices, during the four months December 1979 through March 1980. Note the sales dip—a return to normality—at the end of each promotional period. This standard pattern is described in the jargon used by the marketing people em-

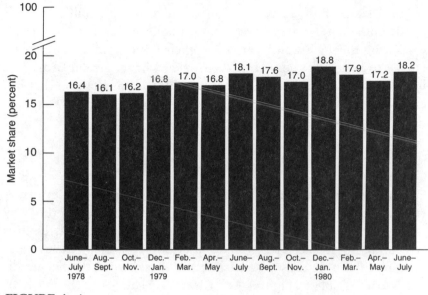

FIGURE A–4
Bimonthly market shares of Brand XA.

ployed by Unilever as the *top hat effect*; the Nielsen chart, when it measures a promotional uplift over a single period, has a profile like a stovepipe hat.

There is not much finesse in how the Nielsen retail audit was able to measure the effect of promotions, but such an effect was certainly detectable in many cases. But as I have stated, advertising was not so measurable—which is something that had an unfortunate consequence.

Analysts became accustomed to finding so little relation between advertising and sales that some advertisers and agencies began to believe that there was no short-term effect to be measured. A doctrine was formulated, which in many quarters is believed to this day, that the sole purpose of advertising is to strengthen the brand image, by reinforcing a brand's nonfunctional added values.[6] In other words, advertising provides only a long-term benefit, not a short-term one. Advertising often does have a long-term effect. But a doctrine focusing on long-term effects is seriously incomplete. This book is concerned with demonstrating that advertising is capable of stimulating sales strongly in the short term. What is more, unless there is a short-term effect, there will be no long-term one.

For lack of any demonstration of advertising's ability to sell goods immediately after its exposure, I believe that many advertisers during the 1980s and 1990s lost their faith in advertising as an engine to generate sales. This led to what I have termed "Advertising's Crisis of Confidence": a major problem of perception that has caused stagnation in the advertising industry during the past decade, both in the United States and abroad.[7]

The Arrival of Scanner Data

Scanner research produces its numbers every week. This information can be recomputed over bimonthly intervals, and in this way we can compare it to historical Nielsen retail audit data. Figures A–5 and A–6 are derived from scanner-based Nielsen research describing sales of brands YA and ZA; and these two diagrams are directly comparable to Figures A–2 (Brand XA) and A–3 (Brand XB).

The sales movements for Brands XA, XB, YA, and ZA are more similar than dissimilar. All four brands have a pronounced seasonality, although the dip from peak to trough is rather greater for YA and ZA than it is for XA and XB. And YA and ZA peak in the win-

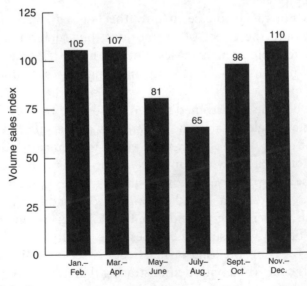

FIGURE A–5
Bimonthly sales of Brand YA (Index: based on sales in first week).

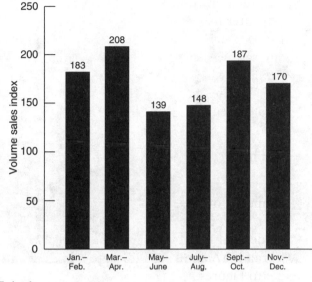

FIGURE A–6
Bimonthly sales of Brand ZA (Index: based on sales in first week).

ter; XA and XB, in the summer. But the point I again want to emphasize is the predictability of the transition from two-month period to two-month period. The only reversals of course are the seasonal ones. All four examples reinforce the impression that markets do not move erratically. There is a similar regularity of patterns in them all.

If scanner data had been presented in bimonthly and not weekly intervals, our perceptions would remain today the same as they were before the 1980s. We would still believe that markets and brands do not change much, and that any changes are regular in the medium term and gradual in the long term. If this belief had been perpetuated, we would be continuing to receive an extraordinary misperception and oversimplification of the real world. Weekly data from scanner research make it abundantly clear that when we look at sales from an extremely short-term point of view, there is nothing short of ferment: rapid rises and falls and frequent changes of direction.

Examine the weekly data in Figure A–7 and compare them with the bimonthly data for the same brand in Figure A–5.

Figure A–7 shows a typical pattern of extreme volatility. The

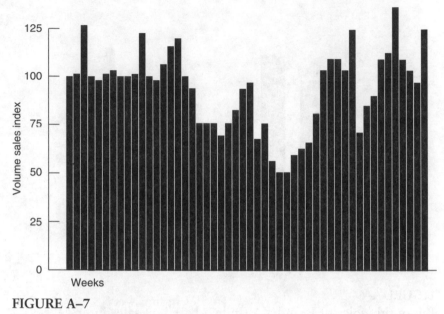

Weeks

FIGURE A–7
Weekly sales of Brand YA. (Index: sales in first week = 100).

sales level in every week is different from that in virtually every other, and some of the week-by-week swings are extremely pronounced. The drop from seasonal peak to trough is 62 percent, compared with the seasonal dip of 41 percent in the bimonthly figures in Figure A–5.

A similar picture emerges for Brand ZA in Figure A–8; compared this with the bimonthly figures in Figure A–6. Figure A–8, like Figure A–7, shows a restless to-and-fro movement from week to week. And the seasonal drop from peak to trough is again steep—60 percent—compared with the dip of 33 percent when the data are analyzed in bimonthly intervals. Both diagrams show unpredictability in place of the regularity that was such a feature of the bimonthly charts.

The week-by-week variations in Figures A–7 and A–8 are typical of the hundreds of examples that scanner research has generated. They confirm and emphasize the truth of the general principle stated earlier in this chapter that the shorter the period covered by each observation, the more erratic the movements from number to number.

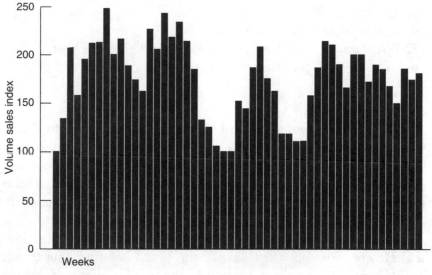

FIGURE A–8
Weekly sales of Brand ZA. (Index: sales in first week = 100).

Of course, the important question we must now confront is: What causes these erratic variations?

Part of the explanation must lie in promotions for the brand we are examining. (The examples of the evaluation of promotional effects which will be found in Appendix C were all derived from week-by-week analyses similar to those in Figures A–7 and A–8). We must also include the influence of promotions for competitive brands, which can cause immediate and temporary sales losses to our brand.

But promotions are not all. As I demonstrated in Chapter 2, advertising can also have a powerful short-term effect, evident from the STAS measure. And we must not forget the advertising for competitive brands, some of which will also have an effective STAS, which may temporarily depress sales of our brand.

There is no doubt whatsoever that when measured weekly, the sales of most brands are volatile, and sometimes extremely so. But the movements are not erratic. They are in response to at least six forces, which do not operate haphazardly:

1. promotions for our brand
2. promotions for competitive brands

3. advertising for our brand
4. advertising for competitive brands
5. distributional problems (e.g., out-of-stock) for our brand
6. distributional problems for competitive brands

Forces 1, 3, and 6 cause sales of our brand to rise; and 2, 4, and 5 cause them to fall.

In the background there are also some longer-term forces at work. Consumer satisfaction with the functional features of our brand will lubricate the short-term effect of advertising and promotions by encouraging repeat purchase. Consumer satisfaction with the functional features of competitive brands will reduce the effectiveness of our own advertising and promotions.

In the short term, sales of any brand constantly change direction. If there are more ups than downs, the brand is on a rising trend; but if there are more downs than ups, the trend is falling. If the ups and the downs balance, we see long-term stability. Markets are not smooth. Transitions are not seamless. But if there is an approximate balance in the forces driving a brand up and driving it down, the eventual result will appear to be smooth and unchanging. Nielsen retail audit figures oversimplified the movements and therefore misled us for years. Scanner research has provided the correction by looking deeper and in more detail at how sales actually move on an individual rather than a cumulative basis.

Nuclear physics provides an analogy, which I hope readers will not consider too fanciful. From the eighteenth to the twentieth centuries, scientists thought that matter, the substance from which the world is fashioned, was made up of collections of tiny solid particles which they called atoms. In the twentieth century, physicists found totally unexpected ways of examining atoms more and more closely. They saw, for the first time, a scene of wonder. Every atom is nothing less than a world in perpetual movement; and each piece of matter—in its complexity and dynamism—resembles a constantly changing universe.

Is the Volatility of Markets a New Discovery?

During the 1980s, a few analysts began to sense instinctively the subtle ways in which markets might be operating. The first release of scanner data provided confirmation and much inspiration.

In 1984, Leo Bogart, who was then head of the Newspaper Advertising Bureau, examined a variety of data (including some based on scanner research) from five large packaged goods fields. He was surprised by what he found. "What appears to be a stable national market for packaged goods is actually extremely volatile. The volatility of purchase volume and brand share parallels what is found in studies of consumer behavior—a constant movement in buying plans and intentions, a constant switching of individual purchase preferences among brands."[8]

Bogart's paper draws many interesting conclusions. One of these has a bearing on a subject I have discussed in this book. When Bogart examined the effect of media exposure, he could trace only a limited sales response to advertising on television and in magazines. But the effect from newspapers was much more directly evident— an outcome he attributed to their promotional orientation: their call to direct action. On the other hand, the other media "work differently and with less immediate and universal impact. Their effects are usually spread through time, absorbed into the dense competitive communications environment, and untraceable, short run, at the point of sale."[9] Note the harmony between Bogart's conclusion about television and magazines and the theory described earlier in this chapter that advertising's effect is exclusively a long-term one.

I believe that there is a more plausible explanation for the apparently more evident effect from newspapers than from other media. The difference is caused by problems of measurement. In Appendix B, in my description of the McDonald study, I make the point that the advertising media were fewer and less complex in Great Britain in 1966 than they are in the United States today. In Britain, it was a relatively easy matter to track household exposure to the advertising for specific brands—in other words, to use the pure single-source method. I believe that this comparison of British and American media conditions holds the clue to an understanding of why Bogart found a greater advertising effect from newspapers than from television and magazines.

Bogart was basing his conclusions on data from a variety of sources. With media that contain as much advertising clutter as television and magazines, traditional research methods lack the precision to isolate the effect of the advertising campaigns for individual brands on the sales of those brands. The marginal effect of the specific campaign is lost in the aggregate effect of all the advertising in these dense and busy media.

But newspapers are a different story. Newspapers carry relatively little advertising for repeat-purchase packaged goods, and most areas of the country have only one or at most two newspaper titles. If we relate consumer purchases in any week to newspaper readership in the same week, there is very little aggregate advertising to confuse the relationship between brand advertising and brand purchase. If we know that a particular brand was advertised in a particular newspaper, we can reasonably assume that people were exposed to that brand's advertising when we measure household exposure to newspapers in general. In other words, we get quite close to the pure single-source research method.

Bogart's discovery of a strong advertising effect from newspapers was the result of his being able to get reasonably close to the crucial relationship of consumer exposure to advertising for a specific brand and purchase of that brand. The fact that Bogart found a positive short-term sales response from newspaper advertising is important. But with a better measurement tool, I believe that he would also have discovered a positive effect from the other media.

Bogart's conclusion about the underlying volatility of markets is echoed in the following comment, which was written at about the same time: "An individual's purchasing behavior may at first glance appear erratic and haphazard. But the more we study such behavior over time, and the more we look at the aggregate behavior of large numbers of consumers, the more regular and predictable it all appears to be."[10]

Appendix B

The History of
Single-Source Research—
The First Steps

T he pioneer work in single-source research was carried out in
Great Britain in 1966. It has become known as the McDonald
study, taking its name from Colin McDonald, the man most responsible for it. Two researchers were in fact involved in planning
this investigation: Timothy Joyce and McDonald, and it is worth
saying a few words about them.

Joyce and McDonald are good examples of the versatile generalists who sometimes emerge from the most traditional type of
British education. Both men were educated in the humanities:
Joyce in Moral Sciences (i.e., Philosophy), and McDonald in
"Greats" (i.e., the Greek and Latin classics). These are often
thought to be effective disciplines to develop a student's analytical
powers, an assumption that is not always ill-founded.

Both Joyce and McDonald began their careers in market research during the 1950s, and it did not take them long to master
the technical aspects of the business. But their nonspecialist liberal
education helped them to look at market research problems in an
open and innovative way, and their mental discipline helped them
focus continuously on the essentials of each problem until they had
found a solution to it. These qualities are what gave birth to the
concept of single-source research.

During the 1960s, Joyce and McDonald were both working at
the British Market Research Bureau (BMRB), the research company owned by the J. Walter Thompson (JWT) advertising agency.
BMRB has been for decades one of the largest and most successful
research organizations in the United Kingdom. It operates indepen-

177

dently from J. Walter Thompson, although the two organizations have many clients in common.

The challenge that Joyce and McDonald faced was a matter of major continuous importance to an agency like JWT: What is the effect of advertising? Most agencies have speculated about this question for decades, and some of them have spent much money trying to find out some answers. Joyce and McDonald (among others) were given the problem, and they began by narrowing down the question into something that could be tackled within the technical limits of market research as it was practiced during the 1960s, at the same time keeping within the budget provided by JWT to cover the cost of the project. They therefore decided to concentrate exclusively on advertising's short-term effect. To go forward in time, a number of findings of operational value emerged from the research, findings which were used on a proprietary basis by JWT on behalf of its clients. This is the reason there was a delay of five years between the original fieldwork and analysis, and McDonald's first publication of the findings.[1]

How McDonald's Research Was Conducted

The tool used for the research was the household diary. In 1966 this was a well-established device widely and productively employed in both the United States and Great Britain. In the 1960s, the only method of collecting diary data was by using pencil and paper: The housewife was required to fill in a diary of her day-to-day purchases. What made the McDonald research unusual was that each respondent was also asked to fill in details of her media exposure—the viewing times of the television programs and commercial breaks she had viewed, and the issues she had seen from a list of thirty-two newspapers and magazines.[2] In 1966, there was only one British television channel running advertising, so it was a simple matter for the tabulators to log the actual brands that appeared on air during the commercial breaks each housewife had viewed. It was also fairly easy to list the brands advertised in the various issues of the thirty-two newspapers and magazines she claimed to have seen.

When McDonald measured advertising exposure, he did not assume that everyone looking at a particular commercial break or at a specific newspaper or magazine actually saw all the advertising in those media. McDonald used the term, common in Britain, of potential exposure to advertising, or Opportunity-to-See (OTS). McDonald measured the number of a brand's OTS immediately before purchase, and this is the number he related to the buying of the brand.

The diary method made it possible to put together within each household the brands purchased by the housewife at any time, and the advertising for those same brands the housewife was exposed to just before she did her buying. In this way the framework for the first single-source research project was established.

For reasons of cost and practicability, the investigation was confined to a single geographical area, London, and to a thirteen-week period. The total sample of households was 255. Nine categories of repeat-purchase packaged goods were covered: bread, breakfast cereals, margarine, milk drinks, shampoo, soup, tea, toothpaste, and washing powder. These varied in their advertising intensity.[3]

The problematical aspects of the research plan were first, that the method of data collection was relatively primitive (by the standards of the 1990s); and second, the scale of the operation was small. The plan of the investigation was nevertheless clean and focused, the whole project was carried through efficiently, and it was subsequently described by McDonald in an impeccable paper.

The greatest innovation of the research was the bringing together, respondent by respondent, of advertising exposure and brand purchasing. This seems in retrospect an obvious way of tackling the question the research was designed to answer. It is nevertheless something that had never been done before. I suspect the reason the research industry had never moved along the path taken by McDonald was because the business was developing in precisely the opposite direction: toward larger size and an increasing aggregation of research data. This made McDonald's move toward disaggregation a startling reversal of the trend.

As I discussed in Chapter 1, none of the single-source research carried out in the United States or anywhere else during the 1980s managed to disaggregate the really important data right down to the individual household. None of it could simultaneously collect the information on advertising exposure for a brand before purchase and actual buying of that brand. This is the system described in Chapter 1 as pure single-source: the method that is at the heart of the Nielsen single-source research on which this book is based.

McDonald's use of the purchase interval is also worth mentioning. Since it encompasses the time between the buyer's last purchase of a brand in the category and her next one, it provides the most precise possible definition of the period during which the short-term effect of advertising should be measured. It also allows for differences between categories and brands, since their purchase intervals differ.

McDonald calculated the influence of advertising on purchase by focusing on buyers and counting those who had changed their brand after having been exposed to advertising for it during the interval since the preceding purchase. He also counted the numbers of people staying with their previously purchased brand after having been exposed (similarly) to its advertising. The main conclusions of the research were however based on brand switching.

Switching is often called brand rotation and it is normal in virtually all categories of repeat-purchase packaged goods, because the majority of consumers have a repertoire of brands they buy with different degrees of regularity. Even if some consumers have not received advertising for a brand, they are likely to rotate their buying to it anyway. But McDonald's precise juxtaposition of the advertising prompt and the subsequent purchase enabled him to measure the extra effect of the advertising in isolation.

When viewed over time, a brand's penetration (i.e., user base) tends to remain constant because the number of people rotating into a brand tends to balance the number rotating out.[4] This tends to keep its market share more or less constant. McDonald's technique measured the extent to which advertising succeeded in generating a net increase of switching into the brand. However, McDonald did not claim that this was a permanent effect; the process of rotation continues after the upward blip stimulated by the advertising. The increase in market share is therefore only temporary.

One problem caused by the use of brand switching was that certain buyers had to be excluded from the tabulations. These were sole buyers (i.e., buyers of only one brand in the category), nonbuyers of the brand being examined, and people unexposed to advertising in the field.[5] These omissions, although necessary, reduced the size of an already small sample.

In my own work with Nielsen data, I have followed McDonald's procedure of relating the respondent's exposure to advertising for the brand to her purchase of it. I have in other words recreated McDonald's pure single-source method. There are however two differences between McDonald's system of measurement and mine, both related to the much larger scale of my own research. See Table B–1. This has caused problems of tabulation because of the complexity of the computer programs Nielsen has to employ.

First (as explained in Chapter 1), I have standardized the purchase interval during which the advertising is measured to the seven days preceding purchase. Second, I do not use brand switching as my means of measuring advertising's effect. I use a measure derived from market share which, as mentioned already in this book, I have called STAS (an acronym for Short-Term Advertising Strength). My preference for this device stems partly from its much greater simplicity; and partly because it is the method I used most often during my professional career. I was always taught to examine advertising's effect by looking for changes in a brand's share of market (SOM). This book is devoted virtually exclusively to SOM, because I have been searching for differences in advertising effectiveness between brands. In this respect my investigation covers different ground from McDonald's. He was most concerned with advertising's average effect across brands. He was not concerned with individual brand variations, although in one of McDonald's earlier papers he presented a narrow range of evidence that advertising effects can vary significantly between brands, at least within one

TABLE B–1
Comparison of McDonald's and Jones's Single-Source Studies

	McDonald	Jones	Approximate Multiplication Factor
Sample size	255	2,000	×8
Time span	13 weeks	52 weeks	×4
Number of categories	9	12	×1.3
Total			×42

product category he managed to explore. This is a tantalizing digression that McDonald was unable to develop because of the limitations imposed by his sample size.[6]

McDonald's Main Conclusions

McDonald was concerned essentially with examining advertising's short-run effect, as demonstrated by data that he averaged. His most important finding, by far, is that advertising can be demonstrated to have such an effect: an effect that operates consistently over all nine product fields covered in the research. The point was made in three separate ways, but was demonstrated with the greatest precision in an analysis of switches to the advertising brand. These data are presented in Table B–2. This table is more complex than it looks, but can be explained by the following four points.[7]

- The table covers brand switches, or occasions in which a change of brand takes place between purchases.
- It percentages the switches to the advertised brand out of the total of all switches into and out of the same advertised brand. Each brand is counted in turn. (This is a very laborious procedure, but it was done for the reason that McDonald was searching for the purest possible measure of advertising effect).
- The two columns compare the effect on brand switching of different quantities of advertising received by respondents.
- Each percentage is an average for all advertised brands in its category.

The higher numbers in the second column show clearly that something happened as a consequence of the larger amount of advertising: this had triggered a consistently higher proportion of brand switching. On average, across all nine categories, the proportion of switches stimulated by two or more OTS was 4.6 percentage points higher than the proportion that followed zero or one OTS. This increase represents a boost of 9 percent (4.6 percentaged on 49.5).

It will strike readers as peculiar that all the figures in Table B–2 are close to 50. The market shares of the brands that were averaged in each product category surely varied much more than this. Mc-

TABLE B–2

Effect on Brand Switching of Two Basic Levels of Advertising Exposure

	Percentage of Switches to Advertised Brand After 0 or 1 OTS	Percentage of Switches to Advertised Brand After 2 or more OTS
Bread	50.2	56.3
Breakfast cereals	49.8	51.3
Margarine	49.9	51.0
Milk drinks	53.7	55.9
Shampoo	47.6	50.0
Soup	49.4	52.2
Tea	48.1	62.8
Toothpaste	47.4	54.7
Washing powder	49.6	52.4
Unweighted average for all categories	49.5	54.1

Donald's data are the direct product of his research method. Since switching into the brand is matched within each consumer's purchasing by her switching out of another brand, 50 percent would be the expected level if advertising had no effect.

This explains also why there is a negative response from one advertising exposure. "The point is again the balance between $0 \rightarrow X$ (switching into the brand) and $X \rightarrow 0$ (switching out of the brand) within each individual. If this is equal, then overall the total, $0 \rightarrow X$ plus $X \rightarrow 0$, across all advertising levels must give a 50:50 result. So if 2 + OTS pushes the $0 \rightarrow X$ percentage above 50, then the other side, 0/1 OTS must balance by being below 50."[8]

The data in Table B–2 provide one of the classic pieces of aggregated evidence that advertising produces a short-term effect. I am however convinced that if McDonald had been working with a statistical sample large enough to break down the category figures, and in particular if he had analyzed advertising response by brand, he would have shown large variability. In the cases of certain brands the response would have been shown to be much greater (and perhaps more immediate) than the averages; and with some brands there would have been no response whatsoever.

Although in the few cases in which McDonald was able to pull out individual brand data, these confirm my hypothesis, that he was in general forced to aggregate his figures by product category. This meant that very important variations between brands were flattened, which effectively masked important truths. This point was discussed in Chapter 4.

Returning to McDonald's main conclusions, the data on continuity of purchase show a similar increase to that shown in Table B–2. These figures demonstrate that advertising at a level of at least two OTS before purchase produces higher amounts of repeat purchase than zero advertising or only one OTS.[9]

McDonald showed that the greatest effect of advertising takes place four, three, or two days before purchase.[10] (This influenced my original decision to concentrate my own study on advertising received shortly before purchase, using a window of seven days prior). McDonald also found directional evidence that exposure levels of advertising in print media have a similar effect to what happens following television. However, since relatively little advertising for repeat-purchase packaged goods appears in print media, the database for examining the response to print advertising is thin.[11]

One or Two Advertising Exposures?

One of the most striking findings of McDonald's research relates to the differential effects of different levels of advertising exposure. The reader has seen in Table B–2 that the exposure data by product category are aggregated into two large groups—brand switches preceded by zero or one OTS and switches preceded by two or more OTS.

If we wish to break these groups down into smaller packets: into individual increments of advertising—zero, one, two, three, four, or more OTS—the subsamples per category are going to become unacceptably small. However, if we total up all nine categories, the advertising exposure data can than be broken down into individual OTS. This is done in Table B–3.[12]

TABLE B–3

Effect on Brand Switching of Small Increments of Advertising Exposure

	Percentage of Switches to Advertised Brand in All Categories (%)
After zero OTS	50.1
After 1 OTS	46.8
After 2 OTS	54.0
After 3 OTS	53.3
After 4 or more OTS	53.7

The rather startling conclusions from Table B–3 are that one OTS has less effect than zero; and that the sales effect peaks at two OTS and thereafter shows no improvement from further advertising.

The findings of Table B–3 had a considerable influence on the advertising industry's concept of media strategy.

Before the publication of McDonald's work in the United States, the notion of Effective Frequency had grown out of the work of analysts such as Herbert E. Krugman, Robert C. Grass, and Hubert A. Zielske. A doctrine was gradually developed that significantly influenced advertising practice. The most persuasive expression of the underlying theory was made by Krugman, when he hypothesized that three exposures of an advertisement are necessary to generate action:

1. The first, to prompt the respondent to try and understand the nature of the stimulus, and to ask the question, "What is it?"
2. The second, to stimulate evaluation ("What of it?") and recognition ("I've seen this before").
3. The third, to remind (and also the beginning of disengagement).[13]

McDonald's work provided an empirical underpinning and strengthening of the doctrine that one advertising exposure is too weak to get through to the consumer.

The explanations by Krugman and the other psychological researchers of why one exposure is not enough are more complicated (and I believe less persuasive) than McDonald's own entirely lucid explanation, which is rooted in common sense.[14] To McDonald, a brand needs two strikes to counteract the advertising of competitive brands. If a number of brands run advertising that is seen by the consumer in the interval before purchase, a brand with two OTS will win over a brand with only one: "It does not mean that one advertising exposure has no effect. It does suggest, however, that as far as short-term stimulating effect is concerned, one exposure tends to be beaten by two or more occurring at the same time, and this could have implications for scheduling tactics."[15] (This is an understatement of what has actually happened). Note in particular McDonald's admission that advertising is capable of having an effect from only one exposure. This is an important point that is underscored by my own research.

In my judgment, the psychological theories are persuasive when explaining the effect on viewers of new campaigns. But for existing and established campaigns, the first two stages—understanding and evaluation—have already taken place when the campaign was first exposed. After it has become part of the scenery, repeated exposures in effect represent reprises of the third stage—the reminding stage—of the communication process. Each advertisement now provides a stimulus for the consumer to buy the brand when she is next in the store. This is my reason for believing that the effectiveness of a single advertising exposure can be explained in terms of the psychological theories, and it is why the data in this book do not refute these theories.

There is no doubt that the psychological theories (which I think were misunderstood), and McDonald's research (which misled because it did not look at individual brands), led the advertising industry in a wrong direction. A hypothesis developed into a concept, which spawned a doctrine, which was transformed into a mantra.

Beginning in the 1960s, advertising agencies, media analysts, and trade press journalists have produced an unending flow of argument and recommendations concerning the amount of advertising frequency necessary to affect sales.[16] One result of all this activity is that standard media planning practice in most American advertising agencies employs flights, or concentrations of Gross Rating Points (GRPs) dense and heavy enough to ensure the average viewer receives two OTS (or more commonly three for safety). Television viewing is distributed in such a way that a substantial minority of viewers receive in practice a much greater weight of advertising than this.

A media policy of this type has unexpected consequences. It is capable of generating great waste. As discussed in Chapter 4, there is evidence that a good deal of advertising works according to a pattern of diminishing returns, that is, with reducing marginal effectiveness as its quantity is increased. In many cases this pattern begins at the first exposure.[17] If a general policy of media concentration results in many advertisers packing their advertising into high-density bursts, it is likely that the extra frequency over the absolute minimum needed for an effect will be operating with very real diminishing returns: in other words, uneconomically.

I believe that the Effective Frequency doctrine, to which McDonald's research added much reinforcement, contributed to a counterproductive and wasteful use of advertising money. McDonald himself is not to be blamed; he described his research from the beginning as nothing more than a small-scale experiment that should be treated with caution.

Nevertheless, a massive multitiered edifice has been built on top of the very small foundation constructed by the psychological theorists and McDonald. One of the purposes of this book is to use additional research to test whether this foundation is able to support everything that has been built on top of it. In particular, I have examined the circumstances when sales may respond to a single advertising exposure. If and when any campaign stimulates such a response, the media budget would be spent most economically by being deployed with minimal concentration and maximum dispersion. In the United States such a doctrine is unorthodox and perhaps heretical.

One of the main findings from the research to which this book is devoted is that advertising effects vary a great deal between brands. This suggests the strong possibility that if some advertising campaigns need two strikes to have an effect, some may not. For brands with effective advertising, media dispersion would certainly be the better strategy.

Appendix C

The History of Single-Source Research— Chasing Hares

The most important technical innovation to influence single-source research—and in effect to lift it off the ground—was the Universal Product Code (UPC). This strip of numbers and precisely printed lines of various thicknesses is an unobtrusive device that can be seen on virtually all packages of consumer goods. It holds exact information that can be read when put in contact with an electronic scanner, a seemingly uncomplicated apparatus that nevertheless employs a laser and a miniature computer. The scanner can either be a fixture on a store's checkout counter or handheld. When the scanner reads the UPC, this instantaneously records the main details of the package—manufacturer, brand name, variety, and size.

The reason the UPC was developed was to increase the efficiency of retailing: to speed the customer through the checkout. Prices are added by the retailer's own computer. Scanners began to come into general use in the mid-1970s, and within a few years they had become the predominant method of ringing sales at cash registers. They are used today for all types of repeat-purchase packaged goods, and most other sorts of product as well.[1]

It did not take long for market researchers to sense the potential of the scanner for collecting research data, particularly for tracking sales on a continuous basis. The two most common research methods for measuring sales to consumers are to count them through the retail store; and to measure them as they enter the household as consumer purchases. These two types of information may appear to be the same. But the main emphasis of the first type is on brands,

189

segments, and categories; in other words, information seen from the manufacturer's point of view. The main point about the second type is that it is concerned with the characteristics of consumers: both their demography and their purchasing patterns.

Before scanners came into use, consumer sales out of the retail store were audited by the method invented by Bev Murphy and introduced by A.C. Nielsen, Sr., during the early 1930s. This method was simple but laborious. A panel of stores was signed up, and the Nielsen researchers would regularly call on each. In order to calculate consumer sales during a defined period (Nielsen worked with two-month intervals), the researchers counted (A) the inventories of a brand within the store at the beginning of the period, (B) deliveries of the brand into the store during the course of the period, and (C) inventories at the end. It was then a simple matter to add A and B and deduct C, to calculate the *disappearance*—which meant essentially the units that had been sold to the consumer—during the interval.

The traditional method of collecting individual data on consumer purchases was to sign up a relatively stable panel of consumers, each of whom would use the pencil and paper home-diary method, described in the discussion of the McDonald study in Appendix B.

The UPC code and the scanner now offered something very much better. Retail sales could be tracked in full detail—a single purchase occasion at a time—from the information collected at the store checkout. By the early 1990s, the new research system had become securely established in the food trade, although the old audit system has only recently been abandoned in drug stores and mass merchandisers. The scanner system, being much simpler than the Nielsen audit method, brought cost advantages by reducing the traditionally very high expense of retail audit fieldwork.

But in addition to the cost saving, sales could now be measured more often. This represented a very major advantage as far as the supply of data was concerned. Weekly figures are now the norm, and there is no substantive reason data collection should not even be done daily. The increase in the amount of data generated has been exponential, but this has brought yet another problem. It has led to a constant stream of complaints from both research practitioners and their clients about the sheer quantity of information generated. Market research departments in manufacturing organizations have often had to be reorganized to deal with it.

Measurement of consumer purchases with scanners also provides a plentiful source of data on consumers' demography and brand-buying habits. But there was an initial glitch in this part of the system. For many years, consumer purchases had to be logged in the store, because handheld scanners were not at first available. Each consumer on the panel was asked to use a plastic card when she passed through the checkout, and this made it possible to keep a record of all the details of her purchases. But the difficulty with this was that the plastic cards were only accepted by some of the stores in the consumer's neighborhood, which meant that there were gaps in the data collection.

There was also the problem of forgetfulness: shoppers not presenting their cards, and cashiers not asking for them at the checkout. The card is sometimes known as a passive system. It is, perhaps, over-passive.

Filling diaries by pencil and paper did at least have the advantage of recording information about all the housewife's purchases no matter where these had been made. But paper and pencil data collection depended on consumers taking the trouble to list accurately all the goods they had bought. This difficulty was eventually solved by the introduction of the handheld scanner. Each panel member could now be equipped with a scanner for use at home to pick up the UPC information from all her purchases. All the Nielsen data on consumer purchasing described in this book were collected in this way.

It is not an exaggeration to say that during the 1980s, the entire business of sales research was transformed by the scanner. Some syndicated scanner services came and went. But two substantial organizations remain, and operate in intense competition with each other: Information Resources Inc. and A.C. Nielsen. The main retail measurement services run by IRI is called InfoScan; Nielsen has ScanTrack.

The consumer panel research run by IRI comprises a national panel, and a test panel called BehaviorScan. This covers eight regions and operates with controlled television exposure: each home in the panel receives identified cable channels, and IRI's clients can vary the advertising weight and/or the copy in each region. The system is therefore geared to market experimentation. In contrast, the Nielsen Household Panel is fully national.

For single-source research, we must of course focus on the consumer panels. These are reasonably efficient in collecting data, bearing in mind the problem of the data gaps when handheld scanners are not used. Nielsen employs them, but IRI still relies on scanners at the store checkout. Despite this imperfection, there is some advantage to the IRI system. It makes it possible to collect a wealth of information specifically related to the retail store, particularly the details of competition between brands. The Nielsen ScanTrack panel of 3,000 stores provides comparable data to the IRI panel. However, ScanTrack and the Nielsen Household Panel are run as separate operations.

Aside from the potential gaps in the collection of the sales data, the most substantial imperfections of all the consumer panels have been that they have been confined to small local areas (no longer true), and there have been problems with the measurement of the media that come into the household. Specifically, none of the systems was able to get to the heart of media measurement by employing what I have described in this book as the pure single-source technique. This was, at least, the situation until the full Nielsen Household Panel service came into operation.[2]

Before looking at some of the uses to which scanner research has been put, it would be useful to itemize the various types of information retail sales research and consumer panel research can provide (see Table C–1). This is a very rich range of possibilities. It offers so many attractive options that the market research industry has spent much time pursuing alluring (and sometimes inconsequential) alternatives. This is why I have entitled this chapter Chasing Hares. There were so many goods in the market research store competing for attention during the 1970s and 1980s that the industry began to lose much of its focus, or at least its interest in advertising effects.

In its early days, scanner research was used most energetically for a purpose that answered a very practical need. But regrettably this involved the first dilution of the single-source concept. The technique was directed at the problem of determining the optimum weight and frequency patterns of television advertising schedules. Scanner research in effect was moved into agency media departments.

TABLE C–1

Types of Research Data Provided by Different Sales Tracking Techniques

Retail Sales Research	Consumer Panel Research
Consumer sales	Consumer purchasing
Trade promotions	Penetration
Consumer promotions	Purchase frequency
Pricing	Purchase frequency distribution
Distribution	
Display	Multibrand purchasing
Competitive brand activity	Repeat purchase
	Consumer promotions
	Consumer demographics
	General advertising exposure (from diluted single-source research)
	Specific advertising exposure (from pure single-source research)

Chasing the First Hare—Media Research

Appendix B described how the concept of Effective Frequency received a new impetus as a result of the McDonald study. Scanner research made an important additional contribution by enabling planners to evaluate accurately the actual OTS achieved against specific user groups. For many years—until at least 1986—this fascinating research device was focused more intently on media planning, buying, and evaluation than on any other marketing problem.[3]

A good way of reviewing the progress of scanner research is to look at the activities of the Advertising Research Foundation (ARF), as recorded in the various publications put out by this organization. The ARF was in the vanguard of the study of Effective Frequency and was the driving force behind the book, published in 1979, that opened up McDonald's work to a wide audience.[4] This book caused much stir and it was followed by a major conference devoted to Effective Frequency held in 1982, at which McDonald participated.[5]

During the 1980s, the ARF began to sponsor conferences in New York specifically concerned with scanner research. In the period 1988 through 1991 alone, five conferences were held that together produced eighty-one papers presented by researchers, advertisers, and advertising agency people.[6] The standard of these papers was understandably variable, but the best of them are even today extremely interesting. Nevertheless, the most striking—and disturbing—feature of the papers is that none of them present data derived from pure single-source research as defined in this book. All the research presented is based on diluted methods.

As a matter of minor interest, the phrase single-source was first used in the mid-1960s in the United Kingdom, and it appears to have been coined by Simon Broadbent, of Leo Burnett. In the United States, the phrase was first employed in 1979.[7]

The eighty-one ARF papers presented between 1988 and 1991 contained much discussion of the media applications of single-source research. Thirty-two papers were based on case studies of different types, and a number of these had a media focus. These demonstrated that all three main suppliers of consumer-based scanner research, IRI and Nielsen plus SAMI-Arbitron (no longer in business), all offered ways of securing the best match between patterns of brand buying and television viewing.[8] The advertisers and agencies commissioning the research obviously wanted to use it to achieve the most cost-efficient media coverage of the users of specific brands.

Which Media? Which Programs?

Tools have been developed to compare the relative value of alternative media (e.g., television and magazines) for different brands. These methods help us to arrive at the best split of the advertising budget between these media, and this division is likely to be different for each brand.[9]

At a more detailed level, finely tuned information can be provided about the detailed coverage of media vehicles, in particular specific television programs. Table C–2 provides an example. The information in this table was presented by Roger Godbeer of Colgate-Palmolive, and in it he compared a number of television programs according to their Brand Leverage Indices: index numbers calculated from estimates of how many users of specific brands watched each show. The basic data were provided by IRI's BehaviorScan.[10]

Table C–2 contains data of very practical value to media planners. St. Elsewhere is the lowest rated of all six shows analyzed, yet it provides the best coverage of users of Brand A. Dallas is the top-rated show, yet it offers above-average coverage only of users of Brand C.

Such permutations of detailed media information are unquestionably valuable for weighting a brand's budget between media vehicles, on the basis of how well they get to its users. And similar data can be used for working out the most efficient regional variations, to improve an advertiser's tactics in the complicated marketplace for spot television.

Knowledge like this—if it were widely used—would have the potential to increase the efficiency of media buying. However, media planning is carried out in a stereotyped and conservative way in many agencies, probably because historical data are regarded as poor predictors of future ratings. Nevertheless, the excellent data provided by diluted single-source research are often neglected. Even then, such information only scratches the surface of what single-source research can provide. And it also introduces a serious problem with priorities.

By concentrating so much scanner research on routine matters

TABLE C–2
Brand Leverage Indices, Primetime Network Programs
Third Quarter, 1984

Program	Nielsen Household Rating	Brand A	Brand B	Brand C
St. Elsewhere	12.6	127	114	86
Cheers	16.8	122	114	95
Hill St. Blues	16.9	115	124	87
Dallas	24.6	103	100	113
Ripley	12.8	95	124	84
Jeffersons	15.7	93	89	124

like assessing program coverage to improve the cost-efficiency of media buying, single-source researchers are effectively diverted from a much more important task. This is to ensure that the strategy on which the buying plan is based is itself well founded. Let me develop this point.

McDonald's original research employed the pure single-source method, but only in a small-scale pilot investigation carried out in a foreign country more than two decades ago. In the United States, McDonald's tentative conclusion was used to support a number of pieces of theoretical and hardly robust psychological analysis. What had started as a hypothesis soon became widely accepted as the Effective Frequency doctrine: something that has become embodied in the media strategy for a huge number of advertised brands. Since the underlying strategic premise is no longer disputed, the advertising industry employs diluted single-source research simply to ensure that this strategy is executed as efficiently as possible.

This approach tackles a minor problem before a major one. I believe it would be more useful for the advertising industry to use single-source research to evaluate—to confirm or deny—the validity of the underlying strategy of Effective Frequency for specific brands. To do this, the sales effects of advertising must be measured case by case. This type of measurement is being neglected because attention is being devoted to the interesting and modestly useful media applications that have occupied so much of the energy and resources of single-source researchers.

When, in 1979, the ARF made a serious proposal to test McDonald's study by conducting a similar piece of research in the United States, the project was abandoned.[11] The research industry was too occupied in chasing a hare. The cleverest people were too busy using their ingenuity to build the most efficient television schedules, which are no more than the best executions of a strategy that is accepted by rote.

Chasing the Second Hare—Retail Research

During the mid 1980s, the focus of single-source research began to change sharply. The technique began to be used increasingly to measure short-term sales effects, but the concentration was on the sales effects of promotions and other instore activities, rather than advertising. The specific research method was the diluted single-source system, and what made this system practicable and indeed simple to use was that the data were collected in retail stores. It became possible to measure accurately the immediate sales from a whole range of specific promotional actions, including their effect on competitive brands. The research was able to trace, in consumer purchasing terms, where the extra business from successful promotions was coming from: from extra purchases by users of the promoted brand, or from users of competitive brands that could be identified.

This represented a large advance on the earlier store auditing system, and I shall shortly illustrate this superiority with a couple of examples. Although it is intrinsically interesting and also valuable to measure the effects of promotions, this is not the focus of this book. I will exercise self-restraint in the extent of the ground I cover here, particularly since the published case study material may not show typical patterns. Indeed the examples published after the various ARF conferences all deal with single brands: individual instances of single-source evaluation. Single cases like these may illustrate more general patterns, but it is certainly not possible on this basis to make confident generalizations about macro effects.

Every type of instore activity can be studied with diluted single-source research, and the various ARF papers include examples of all of the following:

- Test marketing
- Brand segmentation (including the analysis of consumers' brand repertoires)
- Management of manufacturers' brand portfolios
- Retail distribution (including regional variations and analyses of sales in different instore locations)
- Total promotional budgets (including analyses of regional variations)
- Different promotional activities, including the distribution of budgets between alternatives: coupons, instore display, and retail advertising
- Price alternatives, including coupons

I shall stay briefly with the last of the stimuli listed above, and the two cases I shall outline say something about the depth and subtlety of the evaluation techniques used to measure their effects.

Price Optimization

In 1989, a major brand in a large food category increased its wholesale list price by 10 percent. At the same time, SAMI-Arbitron's SamScan was still in the business of measuring retail sales by scanner, and this service was used by a competitor in the same category as the major brand. This competitor was mainly involved in manufacturing store brands, and he wanted to know how to respond to the price increase by the major brand. On the basis of weekly SamScan data covering an eighteen-month period, a number of analyses were made of the price elasticity of the manufacturer's most important store brand, and the cross-elasticities between its different flavors.

Price elasticity is a numerical estimate of the amount by which sales of a brand will fall as a result of a 1-percent increase in its price (and how much they will rise as a result of a 1-percent fall in price). Cross-elasticity measures the effect of price changes on related lines: in this case on alternative flavors of the brand. If the price of flavor A goes up by 1 percent, how much will the sales of B and C go up in response to the fall in the sales of A?

A price elasticity is essentially a measure of substitutability—in other words, competition. The 10-percent increase in the original brand was going to affect the store brand in all events. But it was now important to estimate the effect on sales of the store brand if its price were also increased in turn.

The total research program comprised three stages. First, the elasticities and cross-elasticities were computed. Second, a large number of alternative prices were hypothesized and their overall effects worked out flavor by flavor, and also incrementally, to determine the total effect on the brand. This in turn led to the third step, which was to establish differential—but optimal—price levels for each flavor.

Before the arrival of single-source data, it was very often possible to calculate a price elasticity. The analyst needed enough historical data on different price and sales relationships to calculate averages. But working out a series of interrelated elasticities for a brand's varieties was a different problem altogether. Calculating cross-elasticities was only possible if you did two things: first, track longitudinally (i.e., over time) the consumer sales of each of the flavors; and second, use a number of areas where price experiments could be carried out.

This sophisticated procedure could only be done with the right research tools. "Scanning data was an essential element of this analysis. Thanks to the power which resides in its microlevel measurements (individual stores, UPC, weekly data), it can uncover major opportunities".[12]

Marginal Effects of Alternative Promotions

My second example tells the story of a major manufacturer of household cleaners with a portfolio of three brands. Budgetary pressures were compelling the manufacturer to reduce its promotions, and the BehaviorScan database was used to analyze the relative effects of couponing and certain other promotional activities. The analysis was based on estimates of incremental volume produced by each type of promotion.

For Brand A, coupons added a marginal 2.2 share points. If couponing were abandoned, less than half this business would be absorbed by the manufacturer's other brands, B and C; and more than half would be lost to competitive brands. Trade merchandising added a little less to Brand A: about 2 share points, but if this were abandoned, more than half the lost business would go to Brands B and C. Trade merchandising was therefore the more appropriate activity to cut back.

Similar analyses were made in turn for Brands B and C. The final conclusion was that the reductions in the promotional budget had to be made in different ways. Brands A and B had funds taken out of their trade merchandising; and C had money cut from its couponing budget.

Before single-source research became available, it would have been very difficult to track through the market the effects of changes as small as 2 percentage points of share. This was only possible with a mechanism to trace in detail—purchase by purchase—how much of each brand was bought by individual consumers in response to experimental reductions in specific marketing variables. This had to be a test area program.

As with the first example, it is scanner data that made this type of analysis possible. "Applications such as understanding cross-brand cannibalization and the long-term effects of different marketing strategies require an in-depth understanding of the dynamics of consumer switching and loyalty".[13]

Useful though this sort of research may be, I must reiterate the point that it shifted the attention of the market research profession away from the evaluation of advertising effects. The more uses that were found for diluted single-source data, the less attention was applied to the more difficult job of measuring advertising. There is an obvious and quite sharp trade-off between the two activities which is connected with the ease of evaluating the one and the difficulty of evaluating the other.

One of the most widely publicized features of the marketing business during the past fifteen years has been the shift of emphasis away from advertising toward trade and consumer promotions. Estimates made by Donnelley Marketing show that in 1978, 42 percent of combined advertising plus promotional dollars went to advertising, with 58 percent going into sales promotions. Virtually every year since 1978, the advertising proportion has fallen slightly but inexorably. The most recent estimate for promotional expenditure (for 1993) shows 75 percent of aggregate expenditure going into promotions and only 25 percent into advertising.

There are a number of reasons for this striking trend. But many analysts—myself included—believe that because the sales effects of promotions are relatively easy to measure by diluted single-source research, manufacturers have been increasingly inclined to put more money into promotions. To such manufacturers, sales forecasting appears to have become a simpler and more reliable process than formerly. They have not boosted their expenditure on advertising, because its effects are much more difficult to evaluate. (This of course calls for the pure type of single-source measurement).[14]

However, manufacturers who boost their promotional budgets are blithely unaware of how this action is likely to hurt the profitability of their brands, as well as cause more than one damaging long-term ill-effect.[15] The move of large amounts of money into promotions—with their hidden costs and dangers—does however emphasize very strongly the need to use single-source research to address the effects of the other really important ingredient in the marketing mix. This brings me to what the research business has achieved to date in using single-source research to study advertising.

A Return to Essentials—Measuring Advertising Effects

By the end of the 1980s, the amount of diluted single-source research had been increasing for a decade. By this time, studies like those described in this appendix—and many permutations and variations—were being carried out by virtually all major marketers in the United States. But the use of single-source research to examine advertising effectiveness was still not very advanced.

A limited amount of advertising evaluation was being carried out, although the inability of the research industry to use the pure single-source method put a natural limit on the value of what was done. Out of the eighty-one conference papers published by the ARF between 1988 and 1991, eleven were based on case study material related to advertising. In my opinion these included only two types of study of any real interest, on the basis of their originality and the importance of their conclusions.

Advertising's Contribution to the Marketing Mix

Three ARF papers, relating to three separate brands, presented data that tracked each brand's sales week by week over a year. Each author then attempted, with considerable statistical ingenuity, to evaluate the specific contribution made by every one of the main marketing stimuli.[16]

This evaluation was carried out by regression analysis, a technique discussed in Chapter 1, and one that had been practiced extensively for years before single-source research was first used. Multiple regression is calculated from a large number of statistical observations relating to separate variables, such as specific factors influencing sales, which can then be related to one another. Single source research, even in its diluted form, has been able to generate more statistical information (e.g., from weekly readings and regional data) than was ever before possible. This provides excellent fodder for regression analysis.

The three studies discussed here deconstruct the week-by-week sales of each brand. They estimate the percentage of each week's sales that can be accounted for by variables such as trade promotions, coupons, advertising, and the underlying strength of the brand equity. Each element is peeled away like an onion skin, to provide a remarkably lucid estimate of the individual effect of each of the main sales stimuli.

These week-by-week analyses are then aggregated for the complete year. There are naturally variations among the different cases in the influence of the individual marketing variables; we are looking at different brands. However, one point of commonality between the different studies is that the greatest single influence on a brand's sales is the base equity of the brand. This is a compound of consumers' satisfaction with the brand's functional performance and the added values or psychological rewards that come from repeated use of the brand and the advertising campaign working as mutual reinforcements. It is related to what I mean by a brand's internal momentum, although my concept has a greater element of change built into it.

One of these analyses, covering a year, is shown in Table C–3.

The data in Table C–3 show the short-term influence of advertising to be small but significant. Based on data from general studies of advertising, it is very possible that advertising's contribution at the margin is profitable. It could be paying for itself.[17] The whole analysis is tidy, comprehensible and extremely valuable for the manufacturer of the brand in question. But we should remember that if the pure single-source method had been used in this case to examine advertising, the effect of the latter could have been measured without complex multivariate regression.

TABLE C–3
Relative Importance of Marketing Inputs

Proportion of sales as a result of	Percent
Brand equity	79
Trade effect	13
Coupons	2
Advertising—short-term effect only	6
Total sales	100

Source: The data refer to a year's sales of a food product in Chicago, measured by Nielsen. Andrew M. Tarshis, "Results of the Latest Single-Source Analysis" (ARF Conference, June 1989), 132.

I must re-emphasize the point that we have no proof that the individual cases published by the ARF are typical of the field of repeat-purchase packaged goods as a whole. I am concerned in this book with finding out how many advertising campaigns work and how many do not. This can only be done if we look at numbers of brands. Fortunately, among the ARF conference papers, there is a single collection of interrelated papers that review advertising effects. This collection describes an important and interesting series of pressure-testing experiments carried out by IRI.

The Influence of Increased Advertising Weight

Pressure testing—experimentation with temporarily elevated levels of advertising weight—is a marketing device that has been used for decades. There is anecdotal evidence that one of the leading gasoline marketers in the United States once spent its whole advertising budget for two years in carrying out tests of this type—and with generally inconclusive results. Nevertheless, such tests have often succeeded in swinging the sales needle; sometimes also the profit needle.[18]

Until the publication of the IRI study, the advertising industry had never seen anything as impressive as a collection of 293 tests of increased advertising weight, all assembled in one place. This mass of data was made possible by the area-by-area character of IRI's scanner research.[19]

The most important conclusion from this mine of information was that 49 percent of the 293 tests of boosted pressure managed to generate a sales increase: a rise in sales averaging 23 percent. A positive effect was more common with a campaign change than without one. It was greater when the media reach was increased than when it was not. And it was larger when the category itself was increasing in size than when it was static.

IRI tracked forty-four of their tests to determine whether the original sales increase was maintained after the advertising expenditure had been cut back to more normal levels. The research found a clear long-term effect. Comparing campaigns of increased pressure with those of constant pressure, the heavy-up advertising had a prolonged effect, producing twice the quantity of incremental sales over three years than over one year. The main amount of incremental sales came from increased purchase frequency rather than from higher penetration, and the campaigns did this by persuading irregular buyers to buy more often.

Not surprisingly, the largest relative increases came from small brands, but the largest absolute increases from large ones. IRI also drew interesting conclusions about the relationship between advertising and promotions. Advertising weight tests work best where trade promotional activity is low but the amount of consumer couponing is high. Finally—and not unexpectedly—the research uncovered a deafening disharmony between the copytest scores for the different campaigns and those campaigns' sales results.[20]

I have already explained that my own investigation, which is concerned with brands whose advertising budgets do not change much from year to year, covers different ground from the IRI study. In effect, the two are complementary, and some of the conclusions from the IRI research and my own are mutually reinforcing. But pressure testing by its nature is aggressive; it is carried out with the intention of generating sales increases. This is not always true of ongoing campaigns, especially those for large brands. In most cases, the role of advertising for these is defensive. Advertising's success is not always—or even often—measured by increases in market share. It is more concerned with protecting the status quo, although it sometimes succeeds in increasing slightly the purchase frequency of existing users.

The research in this book nevertheless provides examples of ongoing campaigns that managed to increase brand shares; but it also gives instances of campaigns that succeeded in defending a brand's current position. My examples were discussed in Chapters 8 and 10.

The First Quarter-Century of Single-Source Research

A quarter-century is a long period in the world of market research. Despite the large number of single-source, or at least scanner, investigations that have been carried out in the United States during this time, there are gaps—opportunities for further important work. Here is a summary of the developments that have taken place in the past and some ideas about what needs to be done in the future.

1. Single-source research was first invented as a means of measuring the short-term effect of advertising. McDonald's pioneer experiment, despite its limitations, employed the pure single-source method.

2. McDonald's original work stimulated considerable interest and much discussion, particularly in the United States, but very little further research was actually carried out until the mid-1970s.

3. The introduction of supermarket scanners transformed the situation. At last, diluted single-source research became a practical possibility. But little or no research employed the pure method.

4. As a consequence of the advertising industry's response to the media implications of McDonald's original work, single-source research was applied first to problems of media tactics, in particular to measuring the size of television audiences in order to obtain Effective Frequency.

5. A possible ill-effect of chasing the hare of Effective Frequency is that it may have contributed, and may still be contributing, to the wasteful deployment of advertising budgets.

6. From the mid-1980s, researchers began to use scanner research to measure retail sales and consumer purchases (in effect two sides of the same coin). Most of this research was soon being used to chase a second hare: the evaluation of various types of retail activity, notably promotions.

7. An unexpected and unfortunate side effect of the concentration on retail activity is that it has drawn manufacturers toward promotions, which are easy to evaluate and often demonstrate strong short-term results—although these are mostly unprofitable. Manufacturers have progressively lost interest in advertising, which is difficult to measure and is commonly associated with weak—although often profitable—short-term effects.

8. Single-source researchers have published little aggregated data on the effectiveness of either promotions or advertising. There have been many published examples of individual successes, but it is impossible to generalize from these. The IRI study of 293 advertising pressure tests is a notable exception. But despite its value, it represents an examination of a special case. Pressure test programs are relatively unusual for most brands; and they are getting rarer.[21]

9. There are no aggregated studies of the effectiveness of ongo-

ing advertising campaigns that are exposed at constant weight. This is the particular concern of this book.

10. Once the research industry is able to measure successfully and routinely the short-term effects of advertising, the industry should then address the following interconnected problems:

- How quickly will it be possible to detect campaigns that are not working, and then switch funds to something more productive?
- How easily will we be able to construct a short-term advertising response function for a brand, in order to establish a reliable level of Effective Frequency?
- Will we be able to find out the extent to which advertising and promotions work in cooperation with each other? Can they be planned to work synergistically or must they always conflict?
- How can we better understand advertising's long-term effect? How can we ensure that all campaigns that generate a short-term response will also produce a long-term one?
- How can we use data on advertising's long-term effect to determine accurately advertising's marginal profitability?
- Therefore, will we be able to concentrate on the effective campaigns, and for each of them arrive at the optimal advertising budget, and calculate how best this should be deployed over time?

The research in this book can contribute to answering these questions.

Appendix D

The Logic of the STAS Measure

The Arrow of Effects represents my best effort to describe how advertising works in the short and long term. Look back to Figure 6–2 on p. 64. The STAS Differential provides much of the initial drive to a brand; but it is the synergistic cooperation among three stimuli—positive STAS, price-oriented incentives, and media continuity—that causes the brand to surge, pushed forward by the additional propulsion of its internal momentum.

Although I use words here that imply dynamic movement: *drive*, *surge*, and *propulsion*, brands are almost always fighting competitive battles, so that the surge, drive and propulsion sometimes result in the brand making only modest headway against a powerful tide. But remember that without such positive stimuli, the brand would almost certainly be driven backward.

This book has repeatedly emphasized the importance of STAS. With a positive STAS, a brand can make progress, depending on the strength of its other marketing inputs. But without a positive STAS, a brand is condemned to stagnation in the short term, which is most likely to lead to decline in the long term.

The advertising business has always had difficulty in finding a measure of the short-term effect of advertising. STAS is the most obvious device that common sense can construct. Yet it needed the expensive machinery of pure single-source research to turn this simple concept into a practical measurement tool. This appendix is devoted to what STAS is; also to what it might be thought to be but actually is not.

In the words used in Chapter 2:

- The brand's share of all purchase occasions in the households that had received no television advertising for it during the previous seven days is the *Baseline STAS*.

- The brand's share of all purchase occasions in the households that had received at least one television advertisement for it during the previous seven days is the *Stimulated STAS*.
- The difference between the Baseline STAS and the Stimulated STAS is the *STAS Differential*.

Note the explicit attempt to isolate in a scientific way a single variable—advertising received in the home during the seven days before purchase—and then comparing purchases when that variable is present and when it is not. The design of the STAS measure was meant to focus on the creative effectiveness of a brand's advertising campaign and to allow no complications and exceptions. But is this really what STAS measures?

This appendix looks at two alternative explanations for what STAS might be measuring.

1. Does STAS measure the effect of advertising alone, or advertising plus promotions, or promotions alone? The independent variable in the STAS measure is advertising for the brand received in the home. But homemakers constantly buy promoted as well as unpromoted merchandise, and how does STAS distinguish between the two?

2. Do many brands have skewed demographic profiles? Are the media selected for such brands targeted precisely at the heaviest users and/or the best prospects? In other words, does STAS measure the efficiency of the media buying rather than the effectiveness of the campaign's creative content?

Which Is It—Advertising Alone, or Advertising Plus Promotions, or Promotions Alone?

According to an estimate made by Donnelley Marketing, American packaged goods manufacturers in 1993 spent almost three times as much money on sales promotions as on advertising. Table D–1 gives summarized data for the deal volume in every category covered by this research. In most categories the average is in the 30 to 40 percent range on consumer promotions alone, and for the majority of heavily promoted brands (which are often the most important ones), the percentages are much higher.

TABLE D–1

Purchases on Deal by Product Category

	Volume on Deal (%)	Volume Lowest Brand (%)	Volume Highest Brand (%)
Packaged detergents	38	28	62
Liquid detergents	45	10	62
Bar soaps	35	27	55
Shampoos	31	25	49
Toilet tissue	39	21	56
Ice cream	33	20	48
Mayonnaise	31	12	44
Peanut butter	24	8	40
Ground coffee	38	25	55
Carb. diet soft drinks	40	31	47
Breakfast cereal	39	23	51
Analgesics	23	1	44

Virtually all brands are driven by sales promotions to a substantial degree, and it is therefore to be expected that the STAS effect should generate deal sales as well as nondeal sales. But is it possible that STAS is the driving force for deal sales exclusively? Alternatively, if the STAS influences both promoted and unpromoted sales, does it affect the former more than the latter?

The answer to these questions is no. Table D–2 analyzes all fifty-six brands that have a positive STAS Differential. This table isolates the average share growth that results from different sales stimuli: It is an extension of Table 8–6, which was constructed from the Alpha One brands alone.

The first point that emerges from Table D–2 is that the short-term sales response is marginally greater from the underpromoted brands (STAS Differential of 155) than it is for the heavily promoted brands (STAS Differential of 147). With the Alpha One brands alone, the effect on the sales of heavily promoted volume is more pronounced. (See Table 8–6). STAS drives promotions; and it also

TABLE D–2
Effects of Different Sales Stimuli on All Brands with Positive STAS
Differential

	No. of Brands	Average STAS Differential	Average Share Growth Index
Positive STAS alone	14	155	98
Positive STAS plus above-average adv. intensity	21	117	96
Positive STAS plus above-average price stimulus	12	147	110
Positive STAS plus above-average adv. intensity plus above average price stimulus	9	152	150

drives underpromoted volume. STAS is not exclusively or even pre-
ponderantly a measure of the sales effect of promotions.

As far as the long-term effect of advertising is concerned, promotions contribute a strong synergy. We can infer from Table D–2 that
STAS provides the initial drive, but that the three sales stimuli
working together—positive STAS Differential, above-average
media continuity and above-average promotional expenditure—are
the forces that, in cooperation, drive repeat purchase.

The importance of STAS is confirmed by an analysis of the twen-
ty-two brands which do not have a positive STAS Differential.
Table D–3 takes these brands and examines the average long-term
share growth that results from the same sales stimuli that were examined in Table D–2.

The discussion of the Gamma brands in Chapter 11 explains that
the long-term growth of the more successful Gamma brands was a
result of outside factors unconnected with the advertising. This accounts for Table D–3's index number of 106 for the effect of STAS
plus above-average advertising intensity.

The main conclusion from Table D–3 is that the absence of a
positive STAS Differential has completely inhibited these twenty-
two brands. The importance of Table D–3 lies in the contrast it
makes with Table D–2.

TABLE D-3
Effects of Different Sales Stimuli on All Brands with Negative STAS
Differential

	No. of Brands	Average Share Growth Index
(Negative) STAS alone	7	92
(Negative) STAS plus above-average adv. intensity	11	106
(Negative) STAS plus above-average price stimulus	3	91
(Negative) STAS plus above-average adv. intensity plus above-average price stimulus	1	109

In the pilot work for this investigation, I examined whether the STAS for individual brands of packaged detergents was smaller or greater according to whether households were heavy or light buyers of deal merchandise. (The measure I used to distinguish the heavy deal buyers was whether they bought more than 40 percent of their category purchases on deal).

Table D-4 describes this analysis, and although the subsamples for brands AJ, AK, AL, and AM are small, the effect of advertising on both groups of buyers is very obvious. This table therefore indirectly confirms Table D-2.

The Effect of Efficient Media Buying

Experienced agency media planners are the best people to answer questions about the demographic skews in the use of major brands of repeat-purchase packaged goods, and how these can be matched to the audiences for different television dayparts. The many media planners to whom I have talked are uniformly skeptical about the possibility of using television to exploit demographic selectivity, except in a very rudimentary way. The theory of matching is alluring, but the question we must consider is what practical opportunities are there for buying television spots in complex patterns to parallel the demographic characteristics of brand users?

TABLE D–4
Various STAS Calculations for Packaged Detergents Category

Brand	Overall STAS Differential	STAS Differential for Heavy Deal Buyers	STAS Differential for Light Deal Buyers
AA	97	89	107
AAA	95	86	104
AD	111	108	116
AE	119	144	93
AF	120	100	160
AH	253	247	254
AJ	232	302	133
AK	181	197	137
AL	160	159	164
AM	141	143	141

There are in fact no such opportunities. I could give details of many brands to illustrate this point, but I shall confine myself here to a single and typical example—the breakfast cereal category. Tables D–5 and D–6 are constructed from a recent year's figures from Mediamark Research Inc (MRI). I do not specify the actual year, because I wish to veil the identity of brands LA, LE and LK, so that I am making it difficult for readers to trace them.

The index numbers in Table D–5 compare the buying of the brand by each demographic group with the average of that group in the population; for example, buyers of brand LA in the 18–24 age group are 31 percent below the average for that group in the population as a whole. For brand LA, therefore, the 18–24 age bracket is not a very important target; the population above the age of 54 offers more demographic selectivity.

I chose LA, LE and LK as brands in three different category segments, which are likely therefore to be directed at different demographics. I did this to show the extremes of demographic distribution within the category. But the point that emerges is that there are few such extremes. The only notable example is the low usage of brand LK among the two oldest age groups. LK is in fact a brand

TABLE D–5
Demographic Profiles of Selected Brands of Breakfast Cereal

	LA Buyers' Index	LE Buyers' Index	LK Buyers' Index
All female homemakers	100	100	100
Age:			
18–24	69	70	136
25–34	87	100	178
35–44	103	119	128
45–54	101	118	79
55–64	116	84	31
65 and over	117	90	14
Income:			
$60,000 and more	83	121	102
$50,000–$59,999	100	106	113
$35,000–$49,999	98	113	111
$25,000–$34,999	94	105	124
$15,000–$24,999	110	105	90
Less than $15,000	105	72	77
Region:			
New England	109	129	91
Middle Atlantic	116	119	100
East Central	107	99	94
West Central	102	93	110
South East	101	87	104
South West	99	123	128
Pacific	73	79	76

directed at children and is mostly bought by young mothers. Over-all, there is much more uniformity than irregularity in the patterns. As a general rule, in this and other categories of repeat-purchase packaged goods, there are always fewer users of a brand in any particular demographic group than there are outside that group.

It is also generally true that as a brand grows in size—in particu-

TABLE D–6
Viewing of Television Dayparts by Breakfast Cereal Buyers

	Heavy Buyers Buyers' Index	Medium Buyers Buyers' Index	Light Buyers Buyers' Index
All female homemakers	100	100	100
7:00–10:00 AM	100	105	98
10:00 AM–4:30 PM	93	104	101
4:30–7:30 PM	84	107	103
7:30–8:00 PM	87	107	99
8:00–11:00 PM	91	104	102
11:00–11:30 PM	95	103	102
11:30 PM–1:00 AM	90	106	103

lar as its penetration increases—demographic selectivity falls even further.

If there is a lack of demographic selectivity among buyers of individual brands, this is more than equaled by the lack of selectivity in the composition of the television audience during different dayparts. In Table D–6, the index numbers for each particular daypart measure the viewing of that daypart by heavy/medium/light buyers of breakfast cereals, in comparison with the viewing by the population as a whole. For example, heavy buyers watch the 4:30–7:30 PM segment 16 percent less than the population average. This particular daypart would not therefore be a very efficient way of reaching heavy buyers of breakfast cereals, unless the advertiser bought spots in the time slot at particularly favorable rates.

I could go through a similar exercise to look at cable channels. The amount of selectivity offered by cable is rather higher than that available on the networks, but cable selectivity is more relevant to products with a specialist appeal than it is to mainline packaged goods. Another interesting point about the coverage of cable stations is that, as they grow larger, their selectivity becomes less pronounced. In other words, they begin to resemble the networks.

As we saw with brand buying, television viewing patterns show more uniformity than irregularity. The only general skew in television viewing relates to the television audience itself. If the total audience is set out on a continuum from the heaviest to the lightest viewers, there is high density of viewing at the heavy end. This means that when we increase our purchases of television time, what we really get is even more viewing by heavy viewers: the people who watch the most television already. Heavy viewers are not intensely concentrated into any demographic groups, so that hitting heavy viewers repeatedly is not a very useful way of reaching users of brands that have demographic biases.

My conclusions from Tables D–5 and D–6 do not mean that it is impossible to buy television dayparts selectively; merely that such selectivity is only marginally more efficient than unselective buying. There are differences of emphasis in the consumer buying patterns for any brand that can be matched by parallel differences of emphasis in the television dayparts used for that brand's advertising. But such a matching of patterns—patterns of buying and viewing that have similar degrees of demographic bias—is very far indeed from a 100-percent matching of discrete groups of buyers to discrete groups of viewers.

An interesting additional point regarding efficient media buying appears in Appendix E. I demonstrate there that certain brands can have a stronger advertising presence with their target group than their advertising budgets suggest they should have. The actual advertising presence is measured by Nielsen, and the budgets are estimated by the most prominent media auditing service, Leading National Advertisers (LNA). These brands have an increased share of voice: a higher advertising intensity. This is of course a long-term and not a short-term sales stimulus, and is brought about by efficient media targeting. Efficient media targeting does not influence the STAS measure. But it certainly finds an expression in the long term, because of its ability to impose a stronger advertising presence through building a larger audience at no increased cost.

Should STAS Be Tested Further?

The answer to this question must be yes. But there are practical problems concerned with how it can be done.

This appendix has looked at the influence of the various sales stimuli on deal and nondeal purchases, and at the demographic biases of brand buying and television viewing. In my judgment, these analyses say enough to silence fundamental doubts about the purity of the STAS measure, as far as promotions and demographics are concerned. But there could be further contaminations which have not so far been thought of. What can be done to anticipate these and test their validity?

Because of the possibility of such contaminations, the well-known researcher Timothy Joyce has continuously given me advice about experimenting with the STAS measure. His most imaginative suggestion was that I should compare the STAS figures calculated in the normal way, that is on the basis of purchases preceded by advertising, with their mirror image, purchases followed by advertising. For the latter, a STAS Differential would naturally not be expected—on the assumption that STAS is indeed measuring what it was set out to measure: advertising's influence on purchasing.

Unfortunately, there are two problems with implementing Dr. Joyce's proposal. First, the way in which television time is scheduled in the United States—in compact concentrated flights—means that most purchases that are preceded by advertising are also followed by advertising. We do not therefore have two self-contained groups of purchases, but two groups between which there is an overlap of more than 60 percent.

The second problem with Dr. Joyce's suggestion is that if we try to purify the measures of the STAS image and mirror image, by comparing purchases which are preceded but not followed by advertising, against purchases which are followed but not preceded by advertising, we immediately encounter problems with the size of the subsamples.

These subsamples are in fact reduced to unacceptably small sizes—less than one-sixth of those used to calculate the normal STAS. The samples of purchasing occasions for individual brands are often reduced to numbers smaller than twenty. This causes large and erratic variations in the calculations (as I found when I tried to work out the STAS estimates).

Therefore, at the risk of writing a coda to this appendix that is neither neat nor positive, I must report that the Nielsen sample is not large enough yet to carry out the additional testing which both Timothy Joyce and I believe should be undertaken on the STAS measure. This is therefore a task for the future.

Appendix E

The Calculation of
Advertising Intensity

Chapter 8 describes advertising intensity as follows: It is repre-sented by the brand's share of total advertising in its category (share of voice), divided by its share of market. This produces an estimate of how many percentage points of advertising voice there are for each percentage point of a brand's market share. In this way, we can compare brands of different sizes in accordance with their relative investment in advertising.

If we used share of voice on its own for the calculation, the big brands would automatically be given greater prominence than the small ones. This is the reason for going through the additional piece of arithmetic to calculate expenditure according to share of market.

Nielsen generates a very valuable measure of a brand's advertis-ing exposure—the percentage of category purchase occasions pre-ceded by advertisements for each brand during the preceding seven days. The figures are presented quarterly, and nearly all brands cov-ered by this research were advertised over all four quarters of 1991. These figures formed the basis of my calculation of advertis-ing intensity. I arrived at the estimate for each brand by going through the following three steps, which are illustrated by the data from the bar soaps category in Table E–1.

1. I averaged the figures for the quarterly purchases preceded by advertising exposure, and aggregated the total for the category. This represents the gross duplicated volume of purchases preceded by advertising.

2. On the basis of this total, I calculated each brand's share of voice by simple percentaging. (Strictly speaking, each share repre-sents the brand's share of purchases preceded by advertising. This

is a sensitive and precise, although unorthodox, measure of share of voice).

3. By dividing each brand's market share (first quarter 1991) into its share of voice, I calculated its percentage points of advertising voice for each percentage point of market share. The result is the brand's advertising intensity.

It is interesting to compare the calculations of share of voice in Table E–1 with estimates derived from LNA. The two sets of data appear in Table E–2.

Two points emerge from the comparison of the two research systems.

TABLE E–1
Advertising Intensity Calculation—Bar Soaps Category

Brand	Category Purchase Occasions Preceded by Ads (%)	Share of Voice (%)	Share of Market, 1st Quarter 1991 (%)	Advertising Intensity (%)
CA	20.6	8	15.7	0.5
CB	28.6	11	13.3	0.8
CC	12.7	5	10.4	0.5
CD	25.2	10	5.0	2.0
CE	34.8	14	8.2	1.7
CF	27.8	11	7.1	1.5
CG	11.0	4	5.6	0.7
CH	24.6	10	4.2	2.4
CJ	20.1	8	3.8	2.1
CK	—	—	2.6	—
CL	—	—	0.6	—
CM	—	—	3.1	—
CN	21.9	9	1.0	9.0
CO	7.1	3	3.0	1.0
All Others	17.8	7	16.6	0.4
Total	252.2	100	100.0	

TABLE E–2
Comparison of Shares of Voice—Nielsen and LNA

Brand	Nielsen (%)	LNA (%)
CA	8	7
CB	11	10
CC	5	5
CD	10	13
CE	14	7
CF	11	5
CG	4	in All Others
CH	10	6
CJ	8	7
CK	—	—
CL	—	—
CM	—	—
CN	9	9
CO	3	in All Others
All Others	7	31
Total	100	100

The first point is that the All Others group is much larger in the LNA tabulation. One reason for this is that the smaller brands which comprise the All Others group, use print media more than the named brands do. Print media are audited by LNA but not by Nielsen. Another reason for the difference is that my research is based on special tabulations of Nielsen data. Brands down to a 1- or 2-percent market share were individually tabulated, and less attention was paid individually to the tiny brands that are in the All Others group. The advertising information for these was therefore probably undercounted. This makes no difference at all to the analyses in this book, since my concern throughout is with comparisons between identified brands. Absolute levels of advertising expenditure are not therefore important.

The second point is that for CD, the LNA figure is larger; for

CE, CF, and CH, the Nielsen figures are higher than the LNA ones. These four brands make an interesting comparison. The Nielsen figures relate to buyers' exposure to a brand's advertising (which is why they are used as the basis for the advertising intensity estimates in this book). The LNA figures are based on objective estimates of financial outlay on media space and time. The fact that, for any brands, the Nielsen figures are higher than the LNA ones means that the media targeting of users was very effective for those brands. This is true for CE, CF, and CH. For CD, however, the opposite holds. These examples show that the tactical efficiency of media buying is relevant to the long-term progress of brands.

Appendix F

The Leading Brands in the Product Categories Covered in This Research

Packaged Detergents:
All, Arm & Hammer, Bold, Cheer, Dash, Fab, Oxydol (with Bleach), Purex, Surf, Tide, Tide (with Bleach), Wisk (with Power Scoop).

Liquid Detergents:
Ajax, All, All (Free Clear), Arm & Hammer, Cheer, Cheer (Free), Dash, Era, Purex, Solo, Surf, Tide, Wisk, Wisk (Advanced Action), Yes, Store brands.

Bar Soaps:
Camay, Caress, Coast, Dial, Dove, Irish Spring, Ivory, Jergens Mild, Lever 2000, Pure & Natural, Safeguard, Shield, Tone, Zest.

Shampoos:
Alberto VO5, Breck, Finesse, Head & Shoulders, Ivory, Pert Plus, Rave, Revlon Flex, Salon Selectives, Style, Suave, Vidal Sassoon, White Rain, Store brands.

Toilet Tissue:
Angel Soft, Charmin, Coronet, Cottonelle, Kleenex, Nice 'n Soft, Northern, Scottissue, Soft 'n Gentle, White Cloud, Store brands.

Ice Cream:
Blue Bell, Borden, Breyers, Dreyer's Grand/Edy's Grand, Kemps,

Meadow Gold, Quality Chekd, Sealtest, Turkey Hill, Well's Blue Bunny, Store brands.

Mayonnaise:
Blue Plate, Duke's, Hellmann's/Best Foods, Hellmann's (Light), JFG, Kraft, Weight Watchers, Store brands.

Peanut Butter:
Adams, Jif, Laura Scudders, Peter Pan, Simply Jif, Skippy, Smucker's, Store brands, Generics.

Ground Coffee:
Chase & Sanborn, Chock Full o' Nuts, Eight O'Clock, Folger's, High Yield, Hills Bros, Master Blend, Maxwell House, MJB, Yuban, Store brands.

Diet Carbonated Soft Drinks:
A & W, Coca-Cola, Coca-Cola (Caffeine Free), Diet Rite (Caffeine Free), Dr. Pepper, Mountain Dew, Pepsi-Cola, Pepsi-Cola (Caffeine Free), Seven Up, Shasta, Sprite.

Breakfast Cereals:
GM Apple Cinnamon Cheerios, GM Cheerios, GM Honey Nut Cheerios, GM Lucky Charms, GM Wheaties, Kellogg's Corn Flakes, Kellogg's Frosted Flakes, Kellogg's Frosted Mini-Wheats, Kellogg's Fruit Loops, Kellogg's Raisin Bran, Kellogg's Rice Krispies, Post Grape Nuts, Post Premium Raisin Bran, Store brands.

Analgesics:
Advil, Anacin, Bayer, Excedrin, Good Health, Motrin IB, Nuprin, Tylenol, Your Life, Store brands, Generics.

Notes and References

Preface

1. Nigel Hamilton, *Monty: The Making of a General, 1887–1942* (London: Hamish Hamilton, 1981), 193.

Chapter 1

1. John Philip Jones, *What's in a Name? Advertising and the Concept of Brands* (New York: Macmillan-Lexington Books, 1986), 138–40.
2. John Philip Jones, *Does It Pay to Advertise? Cases Illustrating Successful Brand Advertising* (New York: Macmillan-Lexington Books, 1989), 12.
3. James Spaeth and Michael Hess, "Single-Source Data . . . the Missing Pieces", *Fulfilling the Promise of Electronic Single-Source Data* (New York: Advertising Research Foundation Conference, June 1989), 142.
4. Colin McDonald, "What is the Short-Term Effect of Advertising?", in Michael Naples (ed.), *Effective Frequency: The Relationship Between Frequency and Advertising Effectiveness* (New York: Association of National Advertisers, 1979; second edition forthcoming), 86–88.
5. An example of the use of the AMTES system is given in Jones, *What's in a Name?* 163–65.
6. These definitions were provided by J. Walker Smith, Lynn S. Whitton, Alice K. Sylvester, Stephen A. Douglas, Scott N. Johnson, *New Insights into Single-Source Data* (New York: Advertising Research Foundation Conference, July 1988), 16,24,68,76,114. Lawrence N. Gold, Allan L. Baldinger, Brian M. Shea, Blair Peters, Marilyn Henninger/Edward Dittus, Andrew M. Tarshis, James Spaeth/Michael Hess, Beth Axelrad, *Fulfilling the Promise of Single-Source Data* (New York: Advertising Research Foundation Conference, June 1989), 6,28,54,75,86,120,143,171. Joseph R. Russo, *Behavioral Research and Single-Source Data* (New York: Advertising Research Foundation Conference, June 1990), 11.
7. Michael J. Naples, Randall S. Smith, Leonard M. Lodish, Beth Lubetkin, Josh McQueen, Larry Bisno, Horst Stipp, and Andrew Tarshis, *Breakthrough Mar-*

223

ketplace Advertising Research for Bottom Line Results (New York: Advertising Research Foundation Conference, November 1991).

8. Jones, *What's In a Name?*, 263, Endnote 3.

Chapter 2

1. This chapter describes the Nielsen system that produced the data used in this book. However, in 1994, the size of the panel with meters attached to the television sets was reduced from 2,000 to below 1,500.

2. Walter Reichel, the A:S Link, 515 Madison Avenue, New York, NY 10022. Telephone (212) 750-0565. I gave Reichel a copy of my own pilot study of the Nielsen data base, and he remarked on the similarity of my method to his own. I explained how my system was a derivation of McDonald's. Reichel apparently worked out his method from first principles.

3. I have based this analysis on seventy-eight usable brands. I had to reject two brands because their STAS numbers were outliers: figures so high that they were off the map. To include these would have distorted the averages. The two brands are small, and I assume that the freak observations were the result of statistical error.

Chapter 3

1. There are a small number of cases of brands whose index of growth was 100: in other words, no change. I included these in the growing rather than the declining group. My reason for doing this is that in a competitive environment, to hold one's position is a reasonable measure of success. This is especially true of the brands with the higher shares of market, which are in an essentially defensive position: those I have named in this book the Beta brands.

2. This point is elaborated in John Philip Jones, "The Double Jeopardy of Sales Promotions," *Harvard Business Review*, September-October 1990, 145–52.

Chapter 4

1. Herbert E. Krugman, "The Measurement of Advertising Involvement," *Public Opinion Quarterly*, Winter 1966–67, 583–96; Herbert E. Krugman, "Why Three Exposures May Be Enough," *Journal of Advertising Research*, December 1972, 11–14; Herbert E. Krugman, "What Makes Advertising Effective?," *Harvard Business Review*, March-April 1975, 96–103.

2. Seven of these studies are reviewed in John Philip Jones, *What's in a Name? Advertising and the Concept of Brands* (New York: Macmillan-Lexington Books, 1986), 183–224.

3. Laurence N. Gold, "Let's Heavy Up in St. Louis and See What Happens. Determining TV Advertising Effects on Sales through Econometrics," *Addressing*

Day-to-Day Marketing Problems with Scanner Data (ARF Conference, June 1991), 95–106.

4. Twelve of these studies of diminishing returns are reviewed in Jones, *What's in a Name?* 183–224.

5. Gold, "Let's Heavy Up in St. Louis," 104.

6. Jones, *What's in a Name?* 222–23.

7. Colin McDonald, personal communications, Sept. 15 and Sept. 28, 1993.

8. McDonald, personal communication, Sept. 28, 1993.

9. Ibid.

10. See Appendix B, Endnote 6.

11. McDonald, personal communication, Sept. 28, 1993.

12. This specific recommendation was made to me by a very experienced media specialist, Erwin Ephron.

13. Gold, "Let's Heavy Up in St. Louis", 104.

Chapter 5

1. John Philip Jones, "The Double Jeopardy of Sales Promotions", *Harvard Business Review*, September-October 1990, 145–52.

Chapter 7

1. David Ogilvy, *Confessions of an Advertising Man* (New York: Atheneum, 1963 and 1984), 97.

2. James Webb Young, *The Diary of an Ad Man* (Lincolnwood, Chicago: NTC Business Books, 1990), 227.

3. William Bernbach, *Creativity in Advertising—What It Is, and Isn't* (New York: Association of National Advertisers, 1965), 1–2.

4. Leo Burnett, *Communications of an Advertising Man* (Chicago: privately published, 1961), 25.

5. Ogilvy, *Confessions of an Advertising Man*, 98.

6. Burnett, *Communications of an Advertising Man*, 65.

7. Ibid., 272.

8. Ibid., 47.

9. Ibid., 64.

10. Arthur Koestler, *The Act of Creation* (New York: Macmillan, 1969), 335.

11. William Bernbach, *Beware of Arithmetic* (New York: Association of National Advertisers, 1973), 5–6.

12. Alfred Politz, *The Politz Papers, Science and Truth in Marketing Research* (Hugh S. Hardy, ed.) (Chicago: American Marketing Association, 1990), 170.

13. Randall Rothenberg, personal communication, 1993.

14. David Ogilvy, personal communication, October 4, 1993.

15. Koestler, *The Act of Creation*, 91.

16. Ibid., 27.

17. David Ogilvy, *Ogilvy on Advertising* (New York: Crown, 1983), 157.
18. Amil Gargano, *Thoughts on Comparative and Humorous Advertising* (New York: Association of National Advertisers, 1984), 8.
19. David N. Martin, *Romancing the Brand* (New York: American Management Association, 1989), 139.
20. Jerry Della Femina, *From Those Wonderful Folks Who Gave You Pearl Harbor* (London: Pan Books, 1970), 26.
21. Burnett, *Communications of an Advertising Man*, 95.
22. Ogilvy, *Confessions of an Advertising Man*, 96.
23. William M. Backer, *What the Creative Wants from the Researcher* (New York: Association of National Advertisers, 1983), 4.
24. David Ogilvy, *The Art of Writing Advertising* (Dennis Higgins, ed.) (Chicago: Advertising Publications, 1965), 90.
25. Burnett, *Communications of an Advertising Man*, 37.
26. Ogilvy, *Ogilvy on Advertising*, 107.
27. Rosser Reeves, *Reality in Advertising* (New York: Alfred A. Knopf, 1961), 69.
28. Ogilvy, *Confessions of an Advertising Man*, 135.
29. Ibid., 130.
30. Ibid., 132.
31. Alvin Hampel, *It's Never Been Done Before . . . and Other Obstacles to Creativity* (New York: Association of National Advertisers, 1977), 4.
32. Politz, *The Politz Papers*, 142.
33. James Webb Young, *A Technique for Producing Ideas* (Chicago: Crain Communications, 1940 and 1972), 10.
34. Ogilvy, *Ogilvy on Advertising*, 16.
35. Reeves, *Reality in Advertising*, 34.
36. Claude C. Hopkins, *Scientific Advertising* (Chicago: Crain Books, 1966), 225.
37. Burnett, *Communications of An Advertising Man*, 82.
38. Ibid., 187.
39. Politz, *The Politz Papers*, 43.
40. Ibid., 130.
41. Ibid., 147–48.
42. Della Femina, *From Those Wonderful Folks*, 126.
43. Ogilvy, *Ogilvy on Advertising*, 109.
44. David Ogilvy, *The Unpublished David Ogilvy* (New York: The Ogilvy Group, 1986), 77–78.
45. James Webb Young, *How to Become an Advertising Man* (Chicago: Crain Books, 1963 and 1979), 73.
46. Young, *The Diary of an Ad Man*, 181–82.
47. Samuel Johnson, *The Idler*, No. 41.

Chapter 9

1. Table 9–1 shows that the Alpha One STAS Differential is 43 percent larger than that for the Alpha Two brands (2.0 percentaged on 1.4). This is a

weighted calculation. Using the figures in Tables 8–4 and 9–2 gives a smaller difference, but this is based on unweighted numbers.

2. What is known about price elasticities and advertising elasticities is reviewed and discussed in John Philip Jones, "The Double Jeopardy of Sales Promotions," *Harvard Business Review*, September-October 1990, 145–52.

3. Long-term advertising elasticities are discussed in John Philip Jones, *What's in a Name? Advertising and the Concept of Brands* (New York: Macmillan-Lexington Books, 1986), 92–97.

4. John Philip Jones, "Ad Spending: Maintaining Market Share," *Harvard Business Review*, January-February 1990, 38–42.

Chapter 10

1. John Philip Jones, *Does It Pay to Advertise? Cases Illustrating Successful Brand Advertising* (New York: Macmillan-Lexington Books, 1989), 300–02.

2. John Philip Jones, *How Much Is Enough? Getting the Most from Your Advertising Dollar* (New York: Macmillan-Lexington Books, 1992), 28–33.

3. John Philip Jones, *What's in a Name? Advertising and the Concept of Brands* (New York: Macmillan-Lexington Books, 1986), 114,126.

4. John Philip Jones, "Ad Spending: Maintaining Market Share," *Harvard Business Review*, January-February 1990, 38–42.

5. Jones, *Does It Pay to Advertise?* Foreword by Sir David Orr.

6. Jones, *What's in a Name?* 83–87.

7. John Philip Jones, "The Double Jeopardy of Sales Promotions," *Harvard Business Review*, September-October 1990, 145–52.

8. In Table 10–3, the achieved market share is not much different from the first quarter market share. However the Baseline STAS is below the first quarter market share, and there is an 11 percent rise from Baseline STAS to achieved market share. The fact that the first quarter market share is above the Baseline STAS suggests that the positive STAS is actually boosting sales in the first quarter.

9. Emily DeNitto, "Brand Names Learn from Hard Times to Rise Again," *Advertising Age*, April 18, 1994, 3,46.

10. I certainly found this to be true on many occasions during my professional career.

Chapter 12

1. A.S.C. Ehrenberg, *Repeat Buying, Facts, Theory and Applications*, 2nd edition (New York: Oxford University Press, 1988).

2. A.S.C. Ehrenberg and G.L. Goodhardt, *Seventeen Essays on Understanding Buying Behavior* (New York: J. Walter Thompson Company, no date), 6.2–6.3.

3. When Professor Ehrenberg read this chapter, he criticized on technical grounds my use of index numbers to analyze purchase frequency. He recommended the

use of raw data. However, with a substantial number of brands to deal with, I was faced with the problem of comparing purchase frequency across product categories. Such comparisons are difficult because the average frequency differs between categories, so that brands must be compared with one another within their categories. I could see no alternative therefore but to use index numbers to describe each brand's purchase frequency compared to its category average. I believe that a brand with an index of 125 is in a similar position to a brand with the same index in another category, although the purchase frequency of the two brands may be different when measured in absolute terms.

4. In earlier chapters, I had used figures for first quarter 1991 market share; also the average for the second, third, and fourth quarters, to determine a brand's progress over the course of the year.
5. Ehrenberg, *Repeat Buying*, 169–70.
6. It is possible that the difference in the degree of concentration of buying is a result of the Nielsen method of measuring sales in this research by purchase occasions and not by volume. I am not however persuaded that this hypothesis is valid.
7. Ehrenberg, *Repeat Buying*, 42–45.
8. Ibid., 174.
9. Ibid., 177–81.
10. John Philip Jones, *What's in a Name? Advertising and the Concept of Brands* (New York: Macmillan-Lexington Books, 1986), 131–55.
11. Ibid., 64–65.

Appendix A

1. It certainly had one unintended consequence. It generated, or at least fueled, the theory of the product life cycle, one element of which is the dangerous and counterproductive notion that cyclical decline is inevitable. This is a myth that I have discussed in another place. John Philip Jones, *What's in a Name? Advertising and the Concept of Brands* (New York: Macmillan-Lexington Books, 1986), 49–51.
2. Ibid., 85–87. In that context, XA is named Brand R; and XB is named Brand Q.
3. See for instance Anon., "'Old Standbys' hold their own", *Advertising Age*, September 19, 1983.
4. Jones, *What's in a Name?*, 103–29. Analysis based on Ehrenberg's work.
5. Ibid.
6. A good example is Ogilvy's well-known observation: "The greater the similarity between brands, the less part reason plays in brand selection. The manufacturer who dedicates his advertising to building the most sharply defined *personality* for his brand will get the largest share of the market at the highest profit." David Ogilvy, *Confessions of an Advertising Man* (New York: Atheneum, 1963 and 1984), 102.
7. John Philip Jones, "Advertising's Crisis of Confidence," *Marketing Management*, Vol.2 No.1 (1993), 14–24.

8. Leo Bogart, *The Turbulent Depths of Marketing, an Analysis of Supermarket Scanner Data* (New York: Newspaper Advertising Bureau, 1984), 14. I presented some of my own tentative findings from the Nielsen single-source database to a meeting of the Market Research Council in New York City in March 1993. Dr. Bogart was present at this meeting and was interested in my conclusions regarding the apparent stability yet underlying volatility of markets. He subsequently sent me a copy of his own 1984 paper, which had been distributed fairly widely although I had not seen it before.
9. Ibid.
10. Jones, *What's in a Name?*, 105.

Appendix B

1. McDonald's report was published at different times by the Market Research Society (MRS), the European Society for Opinion and Marketing Research (ESOMAR) and the Marketing Science Institute (MSI). Most recently and authoritatively, the paper occupied a prominent part of a book published by the Association of National Advertisers (ANA). The references in these endnotes will be to this source. Colin McDonald, "What is the Short-Term Effect of Advertising?" in Michael J. Naples (ed.), *Effective Frequency: The Relationship Between Frequency and Advertising Effectiveness* (New York: Association of National Advertisers, 1979), 83–103.
2. Ibid., 84.
3. Ibid.
4. John Philip Jones, *What's in a Name? Advertising and the Concept of Brands* (New York: Macmillan-Lexington Books, 1986), 111–12.
5. McDonald, "What is the Short-Term Effect of Advertising?" 90.
6. Colin McDonald, "Relationships Between Advertising Exposure and Purchasing Behavior", *Journal of the Market Research Society* (1970: Report of 1969 MRS Conference), 89–91.
7. McDonald, "What is the Short-Term Effect of Advertising?" 95.
8. Colin McDonald, personal communication, Sept. 28, 1993.
9. McDonald, "What is the Short-Term Effect of Advertising?" 94.
10. Ibid., 100–01.
11. Ibid., 99.
12. Ibid., 96.
13. Herbert E. Krugman, "The Measurement of Advertising Involvement," *Public Opinion Quarterly*, Winter 1966–67, 583–96; Herbert E. Krugman, "Why Three Exposures May Be Enough," *Journal of Advertising Research*, December 1972, 11–14; Herbert E. Krugman, "What Makes Advertising Effective?," *Harvard Business Review*, March-April 1975, 96–103.
14. Alternative explanations for McDonald's main findings are discussed in Jones, *What's in a Name?* 231–35.
15. McDonald, "What is the Short-Term Effect of Advertising?" 97.
16. One of the major contributions to this development was the book edited by

Naples, the details of which are given in Endnote 1. It is also true that this book was published in response to the large amount of interest in the Effective Frequency concept within the advertising industry.

17. Jones, *What's in a Name?* 183–224.

Appendix C

1. The date of introduction of the UPC is mentioned by Ronald L. Lunde, "Using Scanner Data: Folklore and Fact", *Addressing Day-to-Day Problems with Scanner Data* (ARF Conference, June 1991), 206.

2. IRI has a rather rudimentary system for locating the actual brands advertised, based on reports from agencies and from Arbitron. These are then related to household purchases. The system falls short of the Monitor Plus method used by A.C. Nielsen. Michael G. Pailas, "Promotions or Advertising? Identifying a Better Mix" (ARF Conference, June 1991), 142.

3. Laurence N. Gold, "Introduction to the Workshop: a Proper Definition of Terms," *Fulfilling the Promise of Electronic Single-Source Data* (ARF Conference, June 1989), 6.

4. Michael J. Naples (ed.), *Effective Frequency: The Relationship Between Frequency and Advertising Effectiveness* (New York: Association of National Advertisers, 1979).

5. Archa O. Knowlton, Ira J. Schloss, Hubert A. Zielske, Michael J. Naples, Robert J. Schreiber, Clark Schiller, Marvin Belkin, Joseph W. Ostrow, William V. Behrmann, Herbert E. Krugman, James Spaeth, Gabe Samuels, Albert C. Rohloff, Colin McDonald, William J. McKenna, and Gerald J. Eskin, *Effective Frequency: The State of the Art, Current Media Applications, Next Steps from ARF* (ARF Conference, June 1982).

6. *New Insights into Single-Source Data* (ARF Conference, July 1988); *Fulfilling the Promise of Electronic Single-Source Data* (ARF Conference, June 1989); *Behavioral Research and Single-Source Data* (ARF Conference, June 1990); *Addressing Day-to-Day Marketing Problems with Scanner Data* (ARF Conference, June 1991); *Breakthrough Marketplace Advertising Research for Bottom Line Results* (ARF Conference, November 1991).

7. Gold, "Introduction to the Workshop" (ARF Conference, June 1989), 6.

8. Roger Godbeer, "Single-Source—What the Future Holds: Present Limitations and Evolving Opportunities" (ARF Conference, July 1988), 85–92; Andrew M. Tarshis and Arlene Pitts, "Wand and Card Panels: Issues and Emerging Applications" (ARF Conference, June 1990), 49–85; Anna Fountas, "Applications from Arbitron's ScanAmerica Database" (ARF Conference, June 1990), 85–92.

9. Timothy Joyce, "Intermedia Values and Single Source", *Electronic Media and Research Technologies–XI* (ARF Conference, December 1992), 127–40.

10. Godbeer, "Single-Source—What the Future Holds" (ARF Conference, July 1988), 90.

11. Stephen A. Douglas, "How to Measure How Much Frequency is Enough" (ARF Conference, July 1988), 77.

12. Daniel Ray, "In Search of the Optimum Price: A Case Study" (ARF Conference, June 1990), 133–49.
13. Linda Boland, "Using Household Scanner Data to Evaluate Marketing Mix Alternatives" (ARF Conference, June 1991), 54–63.
14. Researchers who have made the same point include Alice K. Sylvester, "Single Source ... Single Force" (ARF Conference, June 1990), 39; Michael G. Pailas, "Promotions or Advertising? Identifying a Better Mix" (ARF Conference, June 1991), 148; Michael J. Naples, "Bringing Advertising's Bottom Line Effectiveness Research Out of the Closet" (ARF Conference, November 1991), 10.
15. John Philip Jones, "The Double Jeopardy of Sales Promotions," *Harvard Business Review*, September-October 1990, 145–52.
16. Marilyn Henninger/Edward Dittus, "Single-Source Data: A Means Not an End" (ARF Conference, June 1989), 83–102; Andrew M. Tarshis, "Results of the Latest Single-Source Analysis" (ARF Conference, June 1989), 119–37; Gian M. Fulgoni, "Market Mix Modeling with Single-Source Scanner Data" (ARF Conference, June 1990), 263–74.
17. Jones, "The Double Jeopardy of Sales Promotions."
18. Ibid.
19. Leonard M. Lodish, "Key Findings from the 'How Advertising Works' Study" (ARF Conference, November 1991), 35–51; Beth Lubetkin, "Additional Major Findings from the 'How Advertising Works' Study" (ARF Conference, November 1991), 35–51.
20. The failings of copytesting are discussed in John Philip Jones, *What's in a Name? Advertising and the Concept of Brands* (New York: Macmillan-Lexington Book, 1986), 131–55.
21. There is evidence of a decline in the popularity of advertising pressure tests. Allan L. Baldinger, "The of State of Test Marketing: Results of an ARF Survey" (ARF Conference, June 1990), 198.

Index

Acknowledgements

My first and deepest thanks go to my wife Wendy, who made three indispensable contributions to this book. First, she transformed my ragged handwritten drafts into a perfectly presented manuscript. Second, she made many suggestions for improving and clarifying the writing, all of which I welcomed. Third, she kept me cheerful during the six months of hard work that I devoted to the actual writing of this book (excluding the many months of thinking beforehand and rewriting afterward).

I am very grateful to the A.C. Nielsen Company for making available the immense volume of empirical data on which this book is based. I want to emphasize the contributions of my three Nielsen friends Dennis Tobolski, Patrick Kung, and Vincent Wong, who generated all the basic tabulations with the use of great statistical skills and unsurpassed knowledge of Nielsen's computer programs. They also reviewed the whole manuscript. This book is dedicated to them.

My warmest thanks also go to a number of friends and acquaintances who gave me help at various times. They are listed below.

Richard Burton, Erwin Ephron, and William Weilbacher went over the whole manuscript and gave me many observations in matters of principle and in detail. These influenced significantly the format of the book.

A number of other friends made wise and thoughtful comments on draft chapters, or gave other help: Leo Bogart, Simon Broadbent, Steve Coffey, Andrew Ehrenberg, Kelly Forrest, Timothy Joyce, Colin McDonald, Michael Naples, and Andrew Tarshis.

I presented some of the pilot findings from this research at various public meetings, where they generated considerable interest.

These meetings included the Canadian Advertising Congress in Toronto, January 1993; a meeting of the Market Research Council in New York City, March 1993; and a conference sponsored jointly by the Nikkei Research Institute and J. Walter Thompson, Japan, in Tokyo, June 1993.

In early 1994, I presented some of the complete findings to Unilever; to Gesamtverband Werbeagenturen (GWA), the German advertising agencies' association; and to the 1994 European Advertising Effectiveness Symposium in Brussels. During the latter part of the year, I presented my data and conclusions to two conferences in New York City sponsored by the Advertising Research Foundation (ARF); and to a conference in Milan sponsored by the International Advertising Association.

About the Author

John Philip Jones was born in Wales in 1930 and graduated in economics from Cambridge University (B.A. with Honors, M.A.)

From 1953 to 1980, he worked in the advertising agency field. This experience included twenty-five years with J. Walter Thompson—as a market research executive in London (1953–1955), advertising account executive in London (1957–1965), account supervisor and head of television in Amsterdam (1965–1967), account director and head of client service in Scandinavia, based in Copenhagen (1967–1972), and account director in London (1972–1980).

He worked with a wide variety of advertising clients, and was most concerned with major brands of packaged goods (Beta brands, to use the language of this book). His responsibilities included many brands marketed by Unilever, Chesebrough-Pond's (before its acquisition by Unilever), Beecham, Gillette, Nestlé, Pan American, Pepsi-Cola, Quaker Oats, and Scott Paper. He was international account director on Lux Toilet Soap (the largest selling bar soap in the world) from 1972 to 1980.

He was extensively involved with advertising education both within and outside the agency. He conducted his last agency seminar in January 1981, just before he became a full-time educator on joining the faculty of the Newhouse School of Public Communications, Syracuse University. He is a tenured full professor, and was Chairman of the Advertising Department in the Newhouse School for seven years.

For three years, he edited the university's interdisciplinary journal of ideas, *Syracuse Scholar*. He was a member of the Mellon Foundation project group which spent two years exploring the connection between liberal and professional education and which published a book, *Contesting the Boundaries* (Syracuse University Press, 1988). He was a member of the Chancellor's Panel on the Future of Syracuse University, which reported following a two-year study in 1986.

He has published widely in the professional press, with articles in the *Harvard Business Review, International Journal of Advertising, Marketing Management,* and many other publications. He has also been responsible for a number of pieces of national journalism. His books, *What's in a Name? Advertising and the Concept of Brands* (1986), *Does It Pay to Advertise? Cases Illustrating Successful Brand Advertising* (1989), and *How Much Is Enough? Getting the Most from Your Advertising Dollar* (1992) are all published by Macmillan-Lexington Books. They are widely used in the advertising profession in the United States and overseas. His books have been translated into German and Japanese.

He is employed as a consultant by many leading consumer goods companies and advertising agencies in the United States and abroad. He also regularly addresses major professional conferences.

In 1991, John Philip Jones was named by the American Advertising Federation as the Distinguished Advertising Educator of the Year. He was a member of the Council of Judges of the Advertising Hall of Fame, 1991–1994. In 1994, he was elected to the National Advertising Review Board.